FASTER HIGHER SMARTER

BRIGHT IDEAS THAT TRANSFORMED SPORTS

SIMON SHAPIRO

**ART BY
THEO KRYNAUW
AND
WARWICK GOLDSWAIN**

annick press
toronto + berkeley + vancouver

Edited by Linda Pruessen
Designed by Sheryl Shapiro

Annick Press Ltd.

We acknowledge the support of the Canada Council for the Arts, the Ontario Arts Council, and the participation of the Government of Canada/la participation du gouvernement du Canada for our publishing activities.

Canada

ONTARIO ARTS COUNCIL
CONSEIL DES ARTS DE L'ONTARIO
an Ontario government agency
un organisme du gouvernement de l'Ontario

Cataloging in Publication

Shapiro, Simon, author
    Faster, higher, smarter : bright ideas that transformed sports / Simon Shapiro ; art by Theo Krynauw and Warwick Goldswain.

Includes bibliographical references and index.
Issued in print and electronic formats.
ISBN 978-1-55451-813-5 (paperback).–ISBN 978-1-55451-814-2 (bound).–
ISBN 978-1-55451-815-9 (epub).–ISBN 978-1-55451-816-6 (pdf)

    1. Sports sciences–Juvenile literature. 2. Sports–Technological innovations–Juvenile literature. I. Krynauw, Theo, illustrator II. Goldswain, Warwick, illustrator III. Title.

GV558.S53 2016   j613.7'1   C2015-905345-5
                                              C2015-905346-3

Published in the U.S.A. by Annick Press (U.S.) Ltd.
Distributed in Canada by University of Toronto Press.
Distributed in the U.S.A. by Publishers Group West.

Printed in China

Visit us at: www.annickpress.com

Also available in e-book format.

Please visit www.annickpress.com/ebooks.html for more details.

Or scan

To my wife, Sheryl. I couldn't have done this without you.
—S.S.

CONTENTS

Look for this icon. It will tell you about videos on the Internet. Use Google and search for Videos using the suggested search words.

INTRODUCTION

"Faster—Higher—Stronger." That's the motto of the Olympic Games, and it's a great one. It captures the idea that humans can and should push themselves to new heights and be the best they can possibly be. But is it possible that the motto is missing something important—a word that can help us not only reach those heights but soar beyond them? Since we can't just change the Olympic motto with the snap of a finger, we gave this book the title of *Faster Higher Smarter*.

When it comes to athletic achievement, "smart" is often overlooked. It shouldn't be. Sure, there are athletes who have a ton of natural talent and athletes who train harder than the rest. And they're amazing. In fact, they often break records, but usually by just a fraction. This book is about people who are even *more* amazing—the innovators whose ideas changed sports by *a lot*.

Some were great athletes. Others were just average. And one was awful (but he sure loved—and changed—two different sports). Some weren't athletes at all. They were scientists and farmers, teachers and security guards, and bright kids who just experimented and discovered things.

But that's only half the story. If you think that sports are fun and science is dull, you have another think coming. Whether the innovators knew it or not, science is the secret behind most of their work. And once you understand the science behind what's going on, you'll look at sports differently.

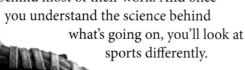

- You'll see the connections between slap shots and pole vaulting, or swimming and ski jumping.

  - You'll know that how you sit on a bike is more important than how hard you pedal.

- You'll see how statistics and analysis can be used to build a winning baseball team.

  - You'll understand how to go over a high jump bar by going under it (kind of).

- You'll appreciate that not all innovations are positive (and that some aren't actually innovations at all!).

When someone comes up with a great new idea, everyone rushes to copy it. Right? Not really! Athletes can be quick or slow to jump on board, depending on how hard it is to change their old habits. And the officials who make up the rules? They're a pretty indecisive bunch. Sometimes they accept the new idea, sometimes they ban it immediately, and sometimes they wait a few years before making up their minds.

But none of that seems to matter. Athletes will always push themselves to be better, whether they are competing in the Olympics or in a local skateboarding contest. Think about how you feel when you're about to play a friendly game of soccer with your friends or swim a few laps in the neighborhood pool. You want to have fun, for sure, but you also want to be the best that you can be. You want to score (or save!) one more goal than you did the last time or shave a few seconds off your time. That desire to improve—to be faster, higher, stronger—is why innovation is here to stay.

CHAPTER 1

HIGH JUMP
THE FOSBURY FLOP

Summer Olympics, Mexico City, October 1968. An energetic crowd turns out to watch the final day of track and field. Although they don't know it yet, they are in for a wild ride. The Olympic Committee declares that the high jump final will start at a height of 6 feet 6 inches. This is quite low for an international competition, and the decision guarantees the crowd a long event—plenty of time, as it turns out, to notice the guy with the awkward-looking style. Instead of running straight toward the bar and jumping over sideways, like everyone else, this athlete runs in a curve and ends up alongside the bar. Then he jumps over backwards, with his head first, landing on his shoulders! And that isn't all: before his run, he rocks from one foot to the other—forward and back, forward and back—for what seems like forever. And why is he wearing one black shoe and one white? At first the crowd laughs whenever he takes his turn, but before long, the laughs turn to cheers, and the crowd knows the strange competitor's name: Dick Fosbury.

In high jump, three failures in a row and you're out. By the fifth round of this competition, five of the 13 finalists are gone, and Fosbury is one of only two jumpers who haven't missed a single jump. Rounds six through

Dick Fosbury on his way to a gold medal in the Mexico City Olympics

eight eliminate another five. Fosbury and his American teammate Ed Caruthers remain, along with Russian Valentin Gavrilov. The nationalities of the final three are no surprise to fans of the sport: since 1887, only American or Russian jumpers have held the world record. All three men make 7 feet 3 inches in round nine. Then Gavrilov fails three times in round 10, with the bar at 7 feet 4 inches. Caruthers makes it on his second attempt, and Fosbury on his first. He has yet to miss a single jump.

Round 11: both jumpers fail their first two attempts at 7 feet 4 inches. Fosbury readies himself for his third try, rocking back and forth, focusing on the jump. Then comes his unique run, curving to the right, and—liftoff!—he sails over the bar with inches to spare. When Caruthers fails his third attempt, the gold medal is Fosbury's—and high jump competitions have a whole new look.

GOOD, BETTER, BEST

Dick Fosbury's strange style took the high-jumping world by storm. By the next Olympic Games, four years later, most high jumpers were using what had become known as the "Fosbury flop." But what did it replace? Before Fosbury captured the imagination of the public and his competitors in Mexico City, there were two other jumping styles.

The SCISSOR JUMP is a simple style where you take off on the outside foot (farthest from the bar) and lift first one leg, then the other over the bar.

Ethel Catherwood training at the 1928 Olympics in Amsterdam. Born in North Dakota, she competed for Canada. Catherwood won the gold medal for high jump.

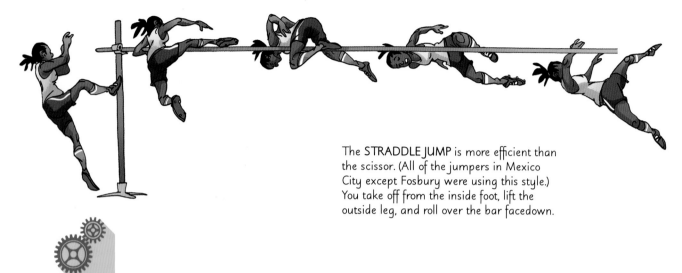

The STRADDLE JUMP is more efficient than the scissor. (All of the jumpers in Mexico City except Fosbury were using this style.) You take off from the inside foot, lift the outside leg, and roll over the bar facedown.

WHY IT WORKS

To complete a successful high jump, you have to tackle two problems:

- ● **get the middle of your body as high off the ground as possible, and**

- ● **arrange all the dangly bits—those pesky arms and legs!—to work to your advantage.**

First things first: height. This part is actually simple. When you jump, you just push off as hard as possible (simple, but certainly not easy!).

Understanding the dangly bits? Not so simple. First you have to know about center of mass. That's the scientific name for "middle of your body." Locating an object's center of mass is easy if we're talking about a simple shape (see diagram). With a block or a ball, the center of mass is right smack in the middle, as you'd expect, but the donut is different. There, the center of mass is located in the hole—not in the actual donut itself.

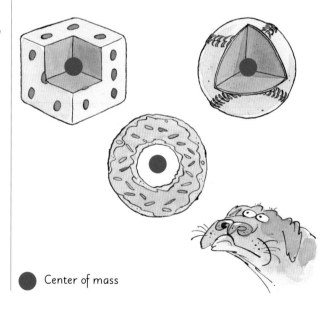

● Center of mass

The **FOSBURY FLOP** is a very efficient jumping style. You take off on the outside foot, twist your body, and go over the bar backwards, arching your back as you do.

Something similar happens with the human body. Your center of mass changes depending on your posture. Stand up straight and your center of mass is in your stomach. Lift your arms and it moves up a little. And if you bend over, your center of mass drops and is located outside your body.

So, suppose you jump hard enough to raise your center of mass to a height of five feet. Does that mean you can clear a bar set at that level? Not necessarily. The height you can actually clear depends on how you arrange those dangly bits—in other words, your jumping style.

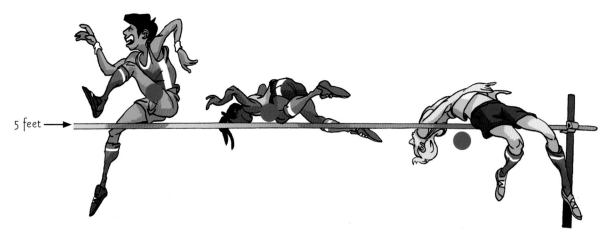

5 feet →

To clear a 5-foot bar with a SCISSOR JUMP, you have to lift your center of mass quite a lot higher than the bar—maybe 5 feet 6 inches.

For a successful STRADDLE JUMP, your center of mass only needs to be a little higher than the bar—maybe 5 feet 3 inches.

Using the FOSBURY FLOP—the "neatest" jumping style of the three—your center of gravity can actually be lower than the bar, maybe 4 feet 10 inches.

IF NOT DICK, THEN DEBBIE

During the same years that Fosbury was developing his technique, Canadian high jumper Debbie Brill had independently started using the same technique. At the age of 16, using her "Brill bend" jumping style, Debbie became the first North American woman to clear 6 feet.

Debbie Brill at the 1984 Olympic Games in Los Angeles

Search for "1968 Olympics high jump" to find videos of Dick Fosbury's jumps.

INVENTING THE FLOP

How did Fosbury come up with this great idea? By accident. Like many athletes, Fosbury had a hard time with the straddle technique. To do it properly, an athlete's timing and coordination need to be perfect—and Fosbury's weren't. In high school, he could only clear 5 feet 4 inches and was struggling in competitions. Desperate for a way to improve his performance, he asked his coach if he could try the scissor jump in the next competition. And that's when everything changed.

"Using the scissors, I make 5-4," Fosbury explained later. "And I am sitting there looking at the bar at 5-6, trying to figure out, 'Now how can I jump higher?' I know I have to lift my butt up, because that is usually where you knock the bar off. So as I try to lift my hips up, my shoulders go back a little bit, and I clear 5-6. It was kind of a lazy scissors. At 5-8, I lift my hips a little higher, and my shoulders go back a little further, and I make it. At 5-10, same thing. By this time, I am going over the bar flat on my back. I'm upside down from everyone else, into kind of a back layout. I go out at 6 feet, and nobody knows what the heck I'm doing."

Fosbury kept using the flop, and in his senior year he placed second in the state high-school championship. But his college coach wasn't a fan of the new technique and kept pushing Fosbury to learn the straddle. Finally, when Fosbury could only manage 6 feet 4 inches using the straddle but broke a school record of 6 feet 10 inches using the flop, his coach said, "We're going to develop this thing."

By 1968, Fosbury had done just that—and nobody ever suggested he try the straddle jump again.

IT'S THE PITS!

Prior to the 1960s, the landing pits for high jump were filled with sand or wood chips. Landing on your shoulders from a height of 7 feet would have been very painful and dangerous. It was only during the 1960s that people started using foam rubber pads, several feet high, in the landing area. So the Fosbury flop wouldn't have been practical—or safe!—until around the time Dick Fosbury invented it.

CHAPTER 2

POLE VAULT
FLEXIBLE FIBERGLASS

Pole vaulting goes way back—way, *way* back. In 500 BCE, Greeks were using spears to vault. And for centuries after, smart people in various cultures used the technique as a shortcut to get across canals or streams without having to walk to the nearest bridge. It's no surprise, then, that the sport made an appearance in the first modern Olympics, in 1896.

In those early days, pole-vaulting athletes pushed themselves to greater and greater heights. But by the 1950s, things had leveled off; it seemed that the sport had reached its limit. Maybe human beings just weren't meant to clear a bar much more than 4.5 meters off the ground.

Or maybe we were. In 1960, something amazing happened. All of a sudden, Olympic pole-vaulters were once again reaching new heights. In 1960, American Don Bragg cleared 4.7 meters, an Olympic record. In 1962, American John Uelses beat the magic "16-feet barrier." That's almost 4.9 meters. In 1964, Fred Hansen hit 5.1 meters. By the 1990s, some athletes were clearing 6 meters! What the heck happened?

REACHING NEW HEIGHTS

The winning heights for Olympic Games between 1896 and 2012. Notice how the heights level off after 1950, but then start to climb again beginning in 1960.

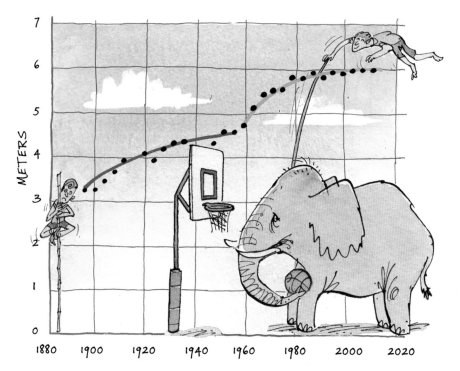

FISHING FOR INSPIRATION

Art Meyers happened. If you've never heard of Art Meyers, don't worry. Most people haven't. But pole vaulting's giant leap forward—or up—owes a great deal to his big idea. Art was no ordinary guy. He never finished high school, and he spent his life working on the family farm, but he was a genius with mechanical things. When he retired, he went to live in Costa Mesa, California, where his son-in-law, Herb Jenks, ran a factory that made fishing poles out of a new material called fiberglass (created by sticking glass fibers into resin sheets and molding them into the desired shape).

Fiberglass is very neat. Light, strong, and flexible, it is perfect for hauling in fish that have no intention of being caught. After a visit to his brother's house in Sherman Oaks—and an afternoon spent watching his nephew practice pole vaulting in the backyard (with a standard metal pole)—Art decided it might be perfect for something else too.

Urged on by Art, Herb Jenks made a vaulting pole out of two tuna-fishing rods and sent it to his young relative. The boy used it to clear 3.3 meters—not bad for a high schooler. The rest, as they say, is history. During a visit to Costa Mesa, athletics coach Virgil Jackson heard about the pole. The next morning, Jackson was waiting for Jenks at his factory. "I haven't slept all night," he explained. "You've got to make those poles and sell them." Jenks did, and Bob Mathias, Jackson's star athlete, used a fiberglass pole during the 1952 Olympics, when he won the decathlon.

A CENTURY OF PREJUDICE

Women's pole vault became an Olympic sport in 2000—104 years after the men's event was introduced. What took so long? Apparently, some men didn't think women had enough upper-body strength to compete at elite levels. American Stacy Dragila probably had something to say about that. In that first Olympic women's event, she had enough upper-body strength to take gold with a height of 4.6 meters. That result would have got her into the finals of the men's competition in the 1964 Olympic Games!

Stacy Dragila setting an American record of 4.75 meters in 2004

13

WHY IT WORKS

Pole vaulting isn't easy; doing it well takes many different athletic abilities. You have to run toward the bar like a sprinter, place the end of the pole accurately in a box on the ground (so that it won't slip), jump like a high jumper, push your body up feetfirst with the strength of a weight lifter, and then twist over the bar like a gymnast. Each of these steps affects how high you can jump, but the pole itself also plays a big part. It's all about energy—and how it's transferred from one form to another.

As the athlete runs, she builds up kinetic energy. That's the energy an object has because of its movement. The faster the object moves, the more kinetic energy it has.

When the athlete plants the pole and bends it, her kinetic energy is changed into elastic energy within the pole. Elastic energy is the kind of energy you store by stretching (or compressing) a spring. The energy is released when the spring is let go, and that's exactly what happens to the pole.

Search for "pole vault Renaud Lavillenie" to find a video of current men's world record-holder.

The athlete goes over the bar, and gravity turns that potential energy back into kinetic energy as she comes speeding down to the mat.

The pole releases the elastic energy, which is then converted to potential energy by pushing the athlete up in the air. Potential energy is the energy an object has because it is above the ground. The higher the object, the greater its potential energy.

HOW HIGH CAN WE GO?

What's next for pole vaulting? Are we going to see world records of 7 or 8 meters any time soon? Don't count on it. The fiberglass pole converts kinetic energy to potential energy very efficiently, so there's not much room for improvement here. Science tells us that the single most important factor when it comes to pole-vaulting success is speed—but the best pole-vaulters are already reaching speeds close to those of world-class sprinters. The world pole vault record is currently 6.16 meters. It was set in February 2014. The previous record of 6.14 meters stood for 21 years!

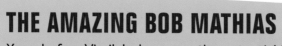

THE AMAZING BOB MATHIAS

Years before Virgil Jackson saw the potential in fiberglass vaulting poles, he saw the potential in his star high-school athlete, Bob Mathias. Here was a guy, Jackson figured, who could tackle the decathlon.

Not everyone can. The decathlon is made for all-around athletes, and it's grueling. It features 10 different track and field events. In the spring of 1948, Jackson urged Mathias to give it a try. "You're already doing the 100 and 400 meters, shot put, high jump, hurdles, and discus," he said. "You'll easily learn the long jump, pole vault, javelin, and 1,500 meters." Mathias was up for the challenge. Three weeks later, the 17-year-old won the decathlon competition at the Southern Pacific Athletics meet in Los Angeles. Two weeks later, he won the nationals, which put him on the U.S. Olympic team. Six weeks later, Mathias, still only 17, became the youngest track and field athlete ever to medal in the Olympics, taking gold in the decathlon. When asked about his plans for the future, his response was, "I guess I'll start shaving."

Mathias won another Olympic gold in 1952, starred in college football, became an officer in the U.S. Marine Corps, acted in Hollywood movies, served four terms as a U.S. congressman, and directed the U.S. Olympic Training Center in Colorado Springs and, later, the National Fitness Foundation. He also served as the president of the American Kids Sports Association.

He believed in the power of sport to improve kids' lives and had a sad comment on the Olympic Games: "Years ago, in the days of the Greeks, wars were postponed to make room for the Olympic Games. In modern times, the Games have been postponed twice to make room for wars."

Bob Mathias on his way to a second Olympic gold medal in the 1952 games in Helsinki, Finland

CHAPTER 3

BASEBALL
TED WILLIAMS AND THE
ART OF SWING SPEED

Ted Williams and his sweet swing

"There goes Ted Williams, the greatest hitter who ever lived." That's what Ted Williams wanted people to say. And lots of people say exactly that.

On Saturday, September 27, 1941, the Boston Red Sox had three games left in the season, all against the Oakland Athletics. Unfortunately, there was absolutely no excitement about where the team would finish—they trailed the New York Yankees by 17½ games. But there was *lots* of excitement about where Ted Williams's batting average would finish. Williams was just above the magic .400 mark (averaging 40 hits for every 100 times at bat). Batting .400 was a rare event in the major leagues, and getting rarer. In fact, no one at all had managed it in the last 10 years. On that Saturday, Williams's average was .401, down from .406 a week earlier.

Red Sox manager Joe Cronin offered to let Williams sit out the last three games in order to protect his average, but Williams refused. He wasn't interested in taking the easy way out. On Saturday, a walk, a double, and three outs dropped his average to .39955. A doubleheader the next day would be his last chance to improve to .400. Could he do it? Even Williams wasn't confident. On Sunday morning, he said, "I went to bed early, but I just couldn't sleep." He was worried about facing a pitcher known for his knuckleball—a pitch that had been difficult for Williams to hit.

Before the first game of the day, Williams's large hands were trembling. On his first at bat, he let two low balls go and then hit a sizzling single to right field. That brought his average up to .40089 and settled his nerves. He proceeded to hit a 440-foot home run, then two singles. He reached base on his last at bat, but the official scorer decided it was a fielder error, making Williams 4-for-5 in the game. That means he got four hits in five at bats. (Read Chapter 16: Statistics for more information on stats like this.) Williams went 2-for-3 in the second game of the doubleheader, which allowed him to finish the season with an amazing .406 average. It's an achievement no major league player has been able to match since— and some say no one ever will. In the same season, Williams also led the league in runs, home runs, walks, slugging percentage (total bases divided by the number of at bats), and on-base percentage. Talk about a terrific year!

WHY WAS WILLIAMS SO GOOD?

Williams worked really hard to be so good. He once told an interviewer, "When I was young, people said, 'Look, he's a natural.' It wasn't that. You've got to *practice*!" Williams also thought hard about hitting. He used to say, "Hitting is 50 percent above the shoulders." He wrote a book called *The Science of Hitting*, which many major league batters still study.

So, what are the secrets to Williams's success? Let's start with the basics: in order to travel as far as possible, the ball needs to come off the bat with as much speed as possible. At the time that Williams was playing the game, everyone knew there were two major ways to get better ball speed: a fast swing and

THE TRAMPOLINE EFFECT

When a bat hits a ball, the two objects touch each other for about 1/1,000th of a second before the ball says "see you later" and takes off. It's too fast to see with the naked eye, but a high-speed photograph shows an amazing picture. The ball gets squashed against the bat before it bounces off and once again assumes its round shape. Most of the kinetic energy (energy of motion) of the ball is changed to sound and heat energy when the ball is deformed.

A wooden bat doesn't get squashed during the impact, but a hollow aluminum bat does. Like a trampoline that gives way and then bounces you higher, the aluminum bat bends a little and springs back into shape, which sends the ball on its way faster than would be the case with a wooden bat. How does this work? It's all about energy: less energy is lost because the ball isn't as deformed. Bending the aluminum bat converts kinetic energy in the ball to elastic energy in the bat, and then back to kinetic energy in the ball. Zoom!

The legendary Babe Ruth in 1920. He used very heavy bats—40 ounces and over. Perhaps he would have been even more amazing if he'd used lighter bats.

a heavy bat. But Williams figured out something new. He realized that of those two, adding speed to your swing was way more important. So he made a decision. Rather than use a heavy bat—as most sluggers did—he used a much lighter one so he could swing it faster. Before Williams had his amazing year, bats of 40 ounces and more were popular. His bat was 33 ounces. Today, most hitters use even lighter bats—about 31 to 32 ounces.

So, speed is more important than weight. But why? Turns out, you simply get "more bang for your buck" (make that "more bang from your bat") by increasing the speed of the bat than you do by increasing its weight. Check out the graph below. It shows how the speed of a baseball coming off a bat is affected when you increase either the weight or the speed. Increasing the bat *speed* by a particular percentage results in a bigger increase in ball speed than increasing the bat *weight* by the same percentage.

There are other advantages to a lighter bat. You can swing it more easily and can therefore wait just a little longer to see the pitch before you need to swing. You can also control it better, so you're more likely to make contact with the ball.

Myrtle Rowe, in 1910. At the age of 18 she played semi-professional baseball on a men's team. We don't know how heavy her bats were. Between 1952 and 1992 women were formally banned from playing in the major leagues.

BAT WEIGHT VS SPEED

The red line shows how the ball speed increases as you increase the *speed* of the bat.

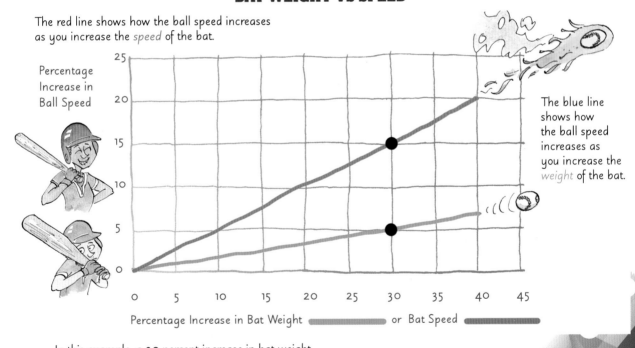

Percentage Increase in Ball Speed

The blue line shows how the ball speed increases as you increase the *weight* of the bat.

Percentage Increase in Bat Weight ▬▬ or Bat Speed ▬▬

In this example, a 30 percent increase in bat weight leads to a 5 percent increase in ball speed. However, the same 30 percent increase in bat speed leads to a whopping 15 percent increase in ball speed.

FAIR GAME

Although college players are allowed to use aluminum bats, they can't use just *any* aluminum bat. As better and better bats were made during the 1970s and 1980s, college batters were scoring too many runs. To keep the balance between batters and pitchers, the authorities have continued to change the rules. Today's college players aren't allowed to use the best bats. They're reserved for youth leagues and recreational players, whose swings haven't (yet!) developed to the point of danger.

BAT BASICS

The physics of a baseball bat whacking a baseball are very complicated. Professor Bob Adair, a physicist who studied the game, once said, "The physics of baseball ain't rocket science. It's much harder." Other than the weight and speed of the bat, some very important considerations are

- the shape of the bat (which can change the location of the center of mass),

- the flexibility of the bat,

- the exact spot on the bat that hits the ball (every bat has a "sweet spot"), and

- the "bounciness" of the ball against the bat (see the Trampoline Effect sidebar).

Baseball started around 1850. Only a few years later, rules about what bats were okay started to crop up. The first came in 1859, when the National Association of Professional Baseball Players Governing Committee specified that bats could be no larger than 2½ inches in diameter. The name of the committee was longer than the rule! And the rules today are still simple: the bat has to be made of a single piece of rounded wood and meet a few considerations for how long and thick it can be. For professionals, pretty much the only change in bats in the last hundred years has been a move from ash wood to maple wood.

College and high-school players, how-ever, have more choices. Manufacturers make hollow aluminum bats that are a lot more effective than simple wooden bats. Balls come off aluminum bats much faster than off wooden ones—so much so that if aluminum bats were allowed in the majors, pitchers wouldn't be safe. A ball hit at them would be traveling so fast that they wouldn't have time to get out of the way—and the impact could be hard enough to kill them. Aluminum bats would also change the flavor of the game: there would be a lot more runs scored, and the hitters would have a definite advantage over the pitchers. Making major leaguers use wooden bats keeps everyone safe and levels the playing field.

Search for "baseball bat slow motion" to find amazing videos of a bat flattening a baseball and of the vibration in the bat.

TRAINING FOR THE PERFECT SWING

If you want to swing the bat as fast as possible, you need to train your body to swing fast. Star hitter José Bautista explains: "Power in baseball comes from the speed of the bat through the zone, which is achieved by becoming stronger, not bigger … people try to get their arms and shoulders stronger to quicken their swing, but that probably makes their swing slower." The essential muscles for speed are found in the torso. Bautista does lots of abdominal work and keeps his core strong with plank exercises.

José Bautista of the Toronto Blue Jays in August 2011. He led the major leagues in home runs in 2010 and 2011.

It's no surprise that soccer players know how to kick. The sport's been around for a long time (longer than football) and its players pretty much do nothing but kick the ball. What *is* surprising is how long it took for football to learn from soccer. Gogolak changed all of that. Once he had success at the professional level, it didn't take long for other teams to catch on. Soon, soccer-style kicks had taken over.

But what is it about the kick that works so well? First, soccer-style kicks are more accurate because your instep provides a bigger surface area than your toe. If your toe

STRAIGHT KICK

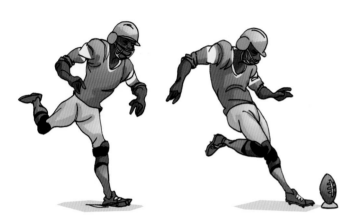

Leg swings straight, connecting with the toe.

SOCCER-STYLE KICK

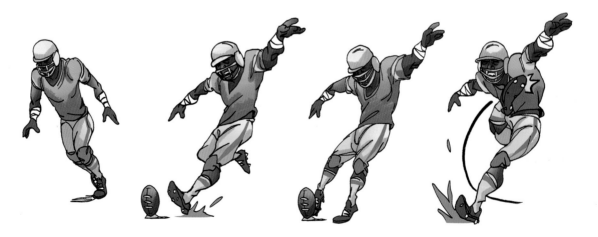

Leg swings around, connecting with the instep.

doesn't connect exactly in the center of the ball, the ball won't go where you want it to go. The bigger instep area isn't so finicky.

Speed is another factor. The faster your foot is traveling at the time it hits the ball, the farther the ball will go. When you're kicking from directly behind the ball, you can only get speed from swinging your leg like a pendulum. Kicking from the side lets you swing your leg in a longer arc and provides more power through the rotation of your hips—a trick that also works when you're swinging a baseball bat (see Chapter 3: Baseball). More power equals more speed, and more speed equals more distance—all of which is good news for kickers!

Search for "field goal kick slow motion" to find videos showing the soccer-style kick being used to kick football field goals.

BAREFOOT BEDNARSKI

Gogolak was the first *famous* soccer-style place kicker. But Fred Bednarski actually beat him to it. Bednarski was five years old and living in Poland when Germany invaded during the Second World War. His family was lucky to survive. They were sent by train—in a cattle car—to a labor camp in Austria, where Bednarski's father was forced to work in a factory. With almost no possessions, the children in the camp played soccer using a "ball" made out of socks. You had to kick it pretty hard to make it go anywhere, and Bednarski learned to kick hard.

After the war, the Bednarski family immigrated to Texas. At school one day, kids were playing a casual game of football and someone invited Fred to try a place kick. He was barefoot and the ball was strangely shaped. But he tried a soccer-style kick and sent the ball 40 or 50 yards—an astonishing distance. The football coach happened to be watching. He called Bednarski over. "You'll come to football practice tomorrow," he said. "I'll get you a pair of shoes."

Bednarski won a football scholarship to the University of Texas. Coach Darrell Royal told his staff, "Nobody mess with Fred! He is a great kicker already, and you don't know anything about soccer-style kicking anyway." Bednarski got great distances in his kickoffs, and in 1957, he kicked the first soccer-style field goal in college football.

BEND IT LIKE BECKHAM

Many soccer players, including superstar David Beckham, are famous for being able to take a free kick and "bend" the ball around a wall of defenders and into the net. The science of making balls curve is the same for any round ball: if the ball is spinning, it will curve in the direction of the spin at the leading edge of the ball. It does this because of airflow.

The diagram below shows a "ball's-eye" view of airflow.

The force that pushes from high to low pressure is called the Magnus force, after the physicist Gustav Magnus. In the 1800s, he figured out why cannonballs curve in the air, but the theory works for soccer balls too.

David Beckham about to bend the ball in 2008. He's playing for the LA Galaxy against FC Dallas.

Search for "Roberto Carlos free kick" to see a video of Brazilian player Roberto Carlos scoring a goal against France in 1997 by bending the ball around a wall of defenders.

Because the ball is rough, it drags a thin film of air with it as it spins.

At point L (low pressure), the dragged air is moving in the same direction as the airflow caused by the movement of the ball—which causes fast airflow.

Faster air movement at L than at H means the air pressure is lower at L than at H (see the Bernoulli Principle on page 29). The result is a force that pushes from H to L, making the ball curve.

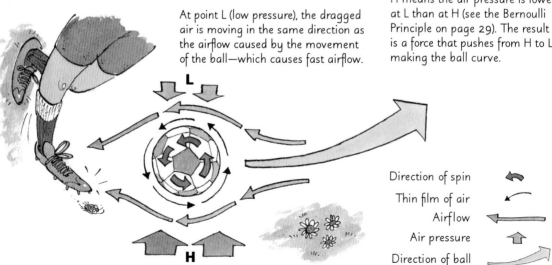

Direction of spin

Thin film of air

Airflow

Air pressure

Direction of ball

At point H (high pressure), however, the dragged air moves in the opposite direction from the airflow. The two flows mix and the airflow slows.

THE BERNOULLI PRINCIPLE

In the 1700s, mathematician and physicist Daniel Bernoulli published his famous Bernoulli Principle. Today, we use that principle to understand how airplane wings achieve lift—and why soccer balls curve. The basics are this: fast-moving air has a lower pressure than slow-moving air.

Okay. So? Lift occurs when the pressure pushing up from underneath an object is greater than the pressure down from above. Check out the illustration of the airplane wing. See that curve on the top? Its job is to force air to move faster over the top of the wing than the bottom. (The air particles moving over the hump need to hurry in order to meet up with the particles moving across the bottom of the wing.)

THE LIFT OF AN AIRPLANE WING

The slower-moving air under the bottom of the wing creates more pressure than the faster-moving air up top. This generates an upward force (dotted arrow), which helps to keep a plane in the air.

Airflow speeds up over the wing.

Airflow

Downward air pressure

Upward air pressure

29

A BRIEF HISTORY OF SOCCER

Football developed in the late 1800s. How old is the game of soccer? Games in which you kick a ball into a goal are probably *way* older than you think. Chinese and Japanese players may have been kicking a ball seven thousand years ago. Certainly the Chinese game of Tsu Chu and the Japanese game of Kemari were played over two thousand years ago. There's even evidence of an international game between the two countries around 50 BCE.

You think football can get a little rough? Legend has it that the first soccer game in England, in the 700s, was played with the severed head of a defeated Danish prince! (Don't even ask if "heading" the ball was allowed.) Soccer became so popular in England that in 1349, King Edward III banned it. It distracted people too much from archery, and he needed good archers for his army. By that point, thankfully, the game had started using a pig's bladder as a ball in place of a severed head, but it was still rough. Teams could consist of thousands of players—one whole town against another. The rules? Kick the "ball" into the opposing village's church. Period. No other rules. People could and did get killed in the chaos.

How about playing in bad weather? For hundreds of years, the Inuit people in the Arctic have been playing *aqsaqtuk*, which means "football on ice." Where there's a will, there's a way!

CHAPTER 5

HOCKEY
THE TERRIFYING
SLAP SHOT

Zdeno Chára, captain of the Boston Bruins, winds up for a slap shot, in 2012. That year, he won the Hardest Shot competition at the NHL All-Star game for the fifth year in a row. His record-setting slap shot was measured at 108 miles per hour.

Imagine standing on the ice in front of a hockey net. An opposing player, 60 feet away on the blue line, arcs his stick backwards and high above his head. He swings it toward you with a deafening crash against the ice. The puck, hard as a rock (well, almost), takes off at over 100 miles per hour. At that speed, it will take 4/10ths of a second to reach your face. How do you feel? Gordie Howe, one of the best players ever, said, "The first thing you thought was, 'Get out of the way.'" That's the slap shot.

So who invented this thing—this bullet that's both feared by goalies and known as a trademark of the game? He's an interesting character. Over a span of 50 years, he played for the Halifax Eurekas, the Africville Sea-Sides, the New York Rangers, the Montreal Canadiens, the Chicago Black Hawks, and the Winnipeg Jets. Well, not really. It's just that there are at least five different players between about 1900 and the 1950s who are said to have invented the slap shot.

The earliest candidate is Eddie Martin, who played for the Halifax Eurekas and the Africville

Sea-Sides in the early 1900s. These were teams in the Coloured Hockey League, which existed in the Maritime provinces of Canada between 1895 and 1925. Hockey was popular in the black communities, which were populated mostly by the children and grandchildren of freed slaves. Black players were never invited to join other teams, so the communities created their own league—and Martin was a star. When his father died, the 23-year-old became the breadwinner for his family. The semi-professional hockey league was a useful source of income.

The most frequently mentioned candidates, however, are Fred "Bun" Cook and Bernard "Boom Boom" Geoffrion ("Bun" because he was as quick as a bunny, and "Boom Boom" because of his booming slap shots). Cook played for the New York Rangers in the 1930s and 1940s. Geoffrion played for the Montreal Canadiens in the 1950s, and he certainly made the move popular. Both players are members of the Hockey Hall of Fame.

"Bun" Cook (left) and "Boom Boom" Geoffrion (right): the leading contenders for "inventor of the slap shot"

A COLORFUL HISTORY

The history of the Coloured Hockey League is interesting and may even hold some clues as to the slap shot's origins. Black players were highly skilled and played a very rough game. They attracted more spectators than the (white) Senior League. In the first (and perhaps only) recorded game between a black and a white team, the black team won 9–7. The Senior League had a rule that didn't allow players to lift their sticks more than waist height on the backswing; the Coloured Hockey League had no such rule. That would have been a key factor in allowing Eddie Martin to develop his powerful (slap?) shot.

The name of one of Martin's teams, the Africville Sea-Sides, was carefully chosen. Not only is Africville a seaside town, but the double S contained a hidden meaning. People who helped slaves escape from the southern United States to Canada were called "Slave Stealers." If they were caught, they were often beaten or even murdered by slave owners. Sometimes slave owners would brand Slave Stealers' faces or hands with a double S to mark them for life. For the black communities in this era, the double S was a symbol of heroism.

Coloured Hockey League players

Finland's Emma Terho scores during a women's match at the 2014 Winter Olympic Games in Sochi, Russia. Notice the flexing of her stick.

Why does a slap shot sizzle? It's natural to think that the way to hit a puck the hardest would just be to hit it cleanly with the stick. But with a slap shot, the fact that the stick slaps the ice before touching the puck is crucial. Here's how it works:

- ◉ **after a big backswing, the stick meets the ice 6 to 12 inches before it touches the puck.**

- ◉ **You bang the blade into the ice surface, bending the stick.**

- ◉ **As you continue with the swing, the stick springs back, providing extra speed to the blade as it hits the puck.**

Sounds easy, right? It isn't. To hit a good slap shot, you need to transfer your weight precisely so that you bend the stick well and then release it at the right time. You must coordinate an arm swing with all of that, too.

Oh, and don't forget, you also have to actually hit the puck!

There's a similarity here with pole vaulting. Remember how the flexible pole takes kinetic energy from the movement of the athlete and turns it into elastic energy, and, finally, transfers it back to kinetic energy once the pole straightens? Well, the same thing happens here. The hockey stick gathers kinetic energy on the forward swing. Then, when the blade connects with the ice, the kinetic energy is turned into elastic energy (stored in the flexible stick). Finally, as the stick straightens, that elastic energy gets transferred quickly back into kinetic energy, and the blade hits the puck at very high speed. The puck, in turn, is launched. Watch out, goalies!

The human eye is too slow to see what's really going on during a slap shot. Search for "slap shot slow motion" to find videos that show how the stick bends and then snaps back before making contact with the puck.

34

A BEND IN THE BLADE

Some innovations happen by accident. In the 1960s, Stan Mikita, a forward with the Chicago Black Hawks, accidentally banged his stick against the boards, bending the blade. Rather than go and get a new one from the locker room, he played with the bent one. He noticed that it actually worked better that way. Now, almost all players use a curved blade.

With a wrist shot, the curve is used to help spin the puck, which helps with stability. Any spinning object has what's called "angular momentum." It's hard to change that momentum, and in many cases, you don't want to! Think of how far a Frisbee can fly. That's because the spinning disk is stable. And it's the angular momentum in spinning bicycle wheels that keeps the bike from falling over. Stability, it turns out, is a good thing!

WRIST SHOT

These arrows show the spinning of the puck.

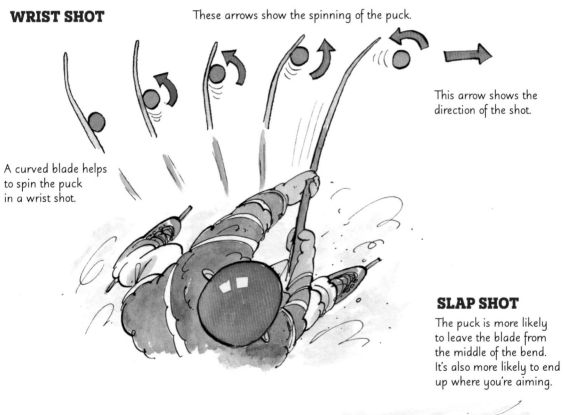

This arrow shows the direction of the shot.

A curved blade helps to spin the puck in a wrist shot.

SLAP SHOT

The puck is more likely to leave the blade from the middle of the bend. It's also more likely to end up where you're aiming.

Some people say that the bend allows a harder slap shot, which isn't true. It does, however, help consistency and accuracy.

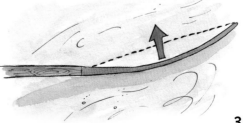

Jacques Plante
in 1960, holding
his trend-setting
face mask

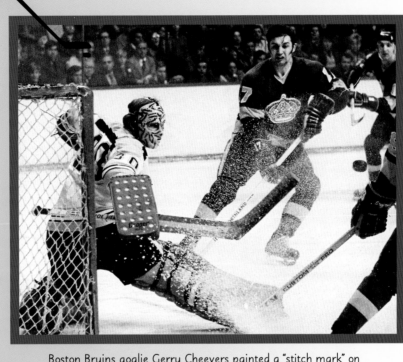

Boston Bruins goalie Gerry Cheevers painted a "stitch mark" on his mask every time a puck hit it in a game. Cheevers and his mask helped Boston win the Stanley Cup in 1970 and 1972.

COVERING UP

Regardless of who invented it, the slap shot is now a standard weapon in hockey. Is it any wonder that, these days, all goalies wear masks? In 1959, Montreal Canadiens goalie Jacques Plante was the first to wear a mask for all games. He had been using one in practice for a while, but his coach wouldn't let him wear it in a game; he was afraid it would block his goalie's vision. But in November of that year, Plante was hit in the face by a shot. After getting stitched up, Plante told his coach that he wouldn't be back on the ice without his mask. The coach caved in.

CHAPTER 6

SKATEBOARDING
OLLIE UP!

Ollie doing an ollie in 1979. Gelfand started skateboarding at the age of 11, and won the South Florida Skateboarding Championship at the age of 13. A year later, he invented the basic ollie, doing it on a sloped or vertical wall.

"Hey, I want to show you a trick this kid's doing on the other side of the park."

In 1977, Stacy Peralta, a top professional skateboarder from California, was touring Florida for *Skateboarder* magazine. The words caught his attention, and fast: he was always interested in seeing new tricks. He followed the stranger, and what he saw changed everything.

"So he takes me to the other side of the park and there's this little kid," said Peralta, remembering that day. "He's about 13 or 14

38

years old. He comes up the other side of the wall and he pops his board, does a 180 in the air, lands on it, comes back down. And it happened so quickly I didn't know what it was. And so I meet the kid and I go, 'What's your name?' And he says, 'My name's Alan Gelfand, but they call me Ollie.' I said, 'What's that trick you just did?' He said, 'Well, they call it the Ollie Pop.' I booked a flight that next weekend, brought him out [to California], and filmed him … A few years later, Rodney Mullen invents the flatland ollie and that changes skateboarding forever … What's beautiful is it's all young kids who did it."

Rodney Mullen invented the flatland (level-ground) ollie and used it to start all his airborne tricks.

Search for "Rodney Mullen." If you haven't seen this guy's tricks before, he'll blow your mind.

No one knows who invented skateboards. They appeared in the 1950s in California, when surfers started attaching roller-skate wheels to wooden planks and "surfing" on sidewalks. By the time Alan Gelfand came along, skateboarders had invented tons of tricks. They had figured out how to lift a skateboard into the air using one foot underneath. But the ollie looked like magic. It still does, the first time you see it. Your initial response is to look for glue or Velcro. How else is it possible to lift a skateboard off the ground while you're standing on it?

But it is possible. The diagrams below will show you how the forces on the skateboard work during the performance of the trick. The weight of the rider and the weight of the board are forces of gravity always pulling straight down. The ground resists a downward force by pushing equally hard straight up. Red arrows show the weight of the rider, orange arrows show the weight of the skateboard itself, and blue arrows show the force of the ground pushing back against the skateboard. Green arrows show the rotation of the board.

Before the start of the trick, the forces are all in balance, so the skateboard doesn't move up or down.

For the start of the trick ...

... stamp hard with your back foot *behind the back wheel*, taking your weight off your front foot. The skateboard rotates counter-clockwise around the back wheel.

Changing your weight now from your back to your front leg would stop the rotation and the board (and you) would be airborne. But waiting a little longer before you change your weight gets you much more height, so wait until ...

... the back of the skateboard bangs hard into the ground. This causes a large reaction force from the ground, which makes the skateboard bounce up into the air.

The board starts to rotate clockwise around the skateboard's center of mass (see Chapter 1: High Jump for more on center of mass).

GIRLS GET IN ON THE ACTION

If you think skateboarding is a guys' sport, think again. Women are awesome at it. In 2013, at age 12, Alana Smith from Mesa, Arizona, became the youngest person ever to win a medal at an X Games. She grabbed silver in the women's skateboard competition in Barcelona. California's Lizzie Armanto is a few years older than Alana and took the gold medal in those games.

Lizzie Armanto (right) and Alana Smith (far right)

Search for "Alana Smith" and "Lizzie Armanto," and be prepared: these videos will shred any idea you might have had about skateboarding being only for boys.

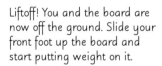

Liftoff! You and the board are now off the ground. Slide your front foot up the board and start putting weight on it.

As the board levels out, put weight on both feet. Gravity brings both you and the board back to earth.

As you come down, bend your knees to absorb the shock of landing.

Sounds complicated, right? It is. You'll need hours and hours of falling-off practice to learn the trick. And don't forget the protective gear—helmets and pads.

X-TREMELY X-CELLENT SPORTS

The X Games started in 1995. If you're looking for more danger and excitement than you find in the Olympics, this competition is for you. X stands for "extreme," and the annual games are certainly extremely popular. They used to be held only in the United States, but there are now X Games in Asia, Europe, and Latin America. If you go in person, you'll find over one hundred thousand buddies taking in the action.

Summer sports include skateboarding, mountain biking, and motocross. Winter sports are skiing, snowboarding, and snowmobile events.

CHAPTER 7

SPEED SKATING SLAPPING ON SPEED

Gunda Niemann-Stirnemann was confident going into the 1997 European All-Round Women's Speed Skating Championship. The all-round competition is brutal—a two-day event comprising four races, from 1,000 meters to 5,000 meters—but Niemann-Stirnemann pretty much owned the title, having won the championship seven times in the last eight years. The German skater wasn't even concerned about the new Dutch "clap skates" she'd been hearing so much about. Actually, she hadn't just heard *about* them—she'd heard them in action too. You couldn't help it. The skates made a nasty clacking sound that disturbed the beautifully quiet scraping of *real* skates.

Maybe Niemann-Stirnemann should have listened more closely. Two days later, young Dutch skater Tonny de Jong used her clap skates to win gold, pushing Niemann-Stirnemann into second

Tonny de Jong during the women's 5,000-meter race at the European Speed Skating Championships in 2002

place. Niemann-Stirnemann was furious. She called for a ban on clap skates and was joined by another famous skater, American KC Boutiette, who also thought using the skates was unfair. He said he wanted to "get a mountain bike, put studs on the tires, and show up with that."

But the skates weren't banned, and suddenly all of the top speed skaters wanted them. Viking, the company that made clap skates, was Dutch and made sure that Dutch athletes were first in line for the new skates. At the 1998 Winter Olympics in Nagano, Japan, Dutch competitors won five of the ten speed-skating gold medals. Even Gunda Niemann-Stirnemann figured "if you can't beat them, join them." She laced up a pair and won a gold and two silver medals. During those same games, all 10 Olympic distance world records were equalled or broken using clap skates.

MEN'S 5K SPEED-SKATING WORLD RECORD TIMES

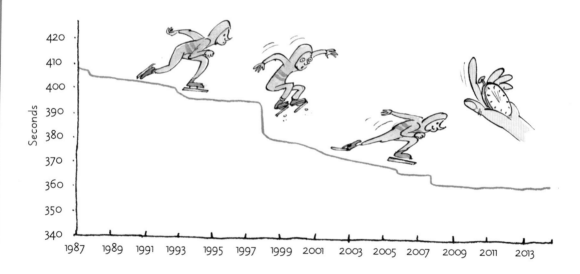

The numbers tell the tale: have a look at the world records for the men's 5,000-meter speed-skating event. Notice how the times—shown in seconds—fall off a cliff when clap skates are introduced at the end of 1997? This is followed by a steady, 10-year decrease as athletes perfect their technique.

CLAP SKATES VS. MOUNTAIN BIKE

Remember KC Boutiette's cranky comment after Tonny de Jong's clap-skate victory? The one where he suggested that a mountain bike with studded tires would give him an advantage over clap skates? He probably should have done some homework before making that claim! The speed-skating world record for 1,000 meters is 66 seconds. The cycling world record for the same distance is only 10 seconds less. But that record was achieved by a trained cyclist on a racing bike on a wooden track designed for bikes to race fast. Would a skater on a mountain bike on ice (even with studs) come anywhere near that time? Definitely not! The smart bet would be on the skater.

DON'T HOLD YOUR BREATH

If you pay attention to the dates in the stories and graphics on these pages, you might wonder why it took more than 10 years for the newly invented clap skate to be used in major competitions. It actually took over *a hundred* years for the invention to be widely used. When Gerrit Jan van Ingen Schenau tried to patent his invention in the 1980s, he was surprised to find that a similar hinged skate had been patented in Germany in 1894! No one knows why the German skate never caught on.

Older people often won't use new inventions, but young people will. Chances are, you're tech support for your parents and grandparents, right? When van Ingen Schenau completed the first clap skates, he gave them to a few elite skaters, all over the age of 25. Although the skaters said they liked the new skates, they chose not to use them in big competitions. After 10 years of this, van Ingen Schenau tried a

new approach: he gave the skates to 11 junior skaters, aged 14 to 18. At the end of the season, the juniors with regular skates had improved their performance by 2.5 percent; the 11 who'd trained on clap skates improved their performance by 6.25 percent. The huge improvement for junior skaters was enough to persuade some senior women skaters to use clap skates in competition.

WHY IT WORKS

In the 1980s, Dutch scientist Gerrit Jan van Ingen Schenau invented what he thought was a new kind of skate. Called the clap skate (or slap skate), it had a hinge that allowed the blade to remain on the ice while the ankle was extended.

Van Ingen Schenau was studying the mechanics of skating. He knew that when you run or jump, you get the maximum power from each step by straightening your knee and extending your ankle. But speed skaters couldn't fully extend their ankles; that could mean catching the point of the skate on the ice, which could either slow them down or cause a fall. The hinge on his new skate solved that problem: the ankle could fully extend while the entire blade remained in contact with the ice. The result? A stronger push at every stroke.

Van Ingen Schenau's theory was right, but there's another big reason why the clap skate is so effective: the ankle and skate make a *lever*. Levers are pretty useful tools. They can take a small force and turn it into a bigger one. But they can also take a big force and turn it into a smaller one. That's what regular skates do—and what clap skates fix.

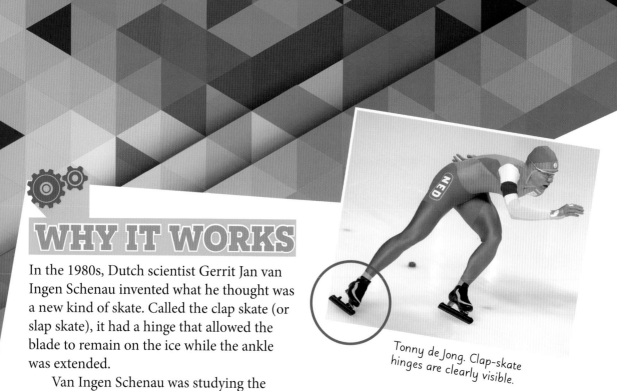

Tonny de Jong. Clap-skate hinges are clearly visible.

A LEVER LESSON

All levers have two important parts: the lever itself and the fulcrum, or pivot point. Let's say a heavy weight is resting on top of one end of a lever, and you are at the other, with the fulcrum somewhere in the middle. You'd be able to lift that weight by pressing down on your side of the lever. The placement of the fulcrum determines how high the weight will move and how much force is required to move it. The farther away from the fulcrum you are, the less force you have to apply. (Over two thousand years ago, Greek philosopher Archimedes said, "Give me a lever long enough and a fulcrum on which to place it, and I shall move the world.") There are three common classes of levers:

CLASS 1

The force you apply (effort) and the force you produce (output force) are on opposite sides of the fulcrum. If the effort is *farther* from the fulcrum than the output force, the output force is greater than the effort. This is an efficient lever. You can use it to lift something much heavier than your effort.

CLASS 2

The effort and output forces are on the same side of the fulcrum, and the effort is *farther* from the fulcrum than the output force. This is also an efficient lever: your output force is greater than your effort.

CLASS 3

The effort and output forces are on the same side of the fulcrum (as with a Class 2 lever), but this time, the effort is *closer* to the fulcrum than the output force is. This is an inefficient lever. Your output force is less than your effort. So your effort needs to be greater than the weight of whatever you're lifting.

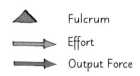

Fulcrum

Effort

Output Force

What does all this mean to a speed skater? Think of the ankle as the fulcrum of a lever, with the effort applied through the ball of the foot. What you're trying to do is to get as much output force as possible from pushing the skate against the ice.

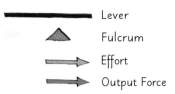

Lever
Fulcrum
Effort
Output Force

The regular skate and ankle form a Class 3 lever. The ankle is the fulcrum, the effort is through the ball of the foot, and the output force is at the end of the blade. This is not an efficient lever. The output force is less than the effort.

The clap skate changes the formation of the lever. The ankle is still the fulcrum and the effort is still through the ball of the foot, but the skate's hinge has moved the output force. That force is now also located at the ball of the foot. And when the output force and the effort are the same distance from the fulcrum, you end up with a lever halfway between an efficient Class 2 and an inefficient Class 3. So, while a clap skate doesn't give you more output force than your effort, it also doesn't give you less, the way a standard skate does.

___

It's pretty much impossible to see clap skates working with your bare eyes. Search for "slow motion speed skating clap skates" to find a video showing clap skates at the start of a race and at the crucial crossover corners.

OTHER INNOVATIONS IN SPEED SKATING

Over the years, speed skating has been very open to technical innovations. In addition to the advances made because of clap skates, big increases in speed have come from using artificial ice on indoor skating tracks and from wearing aerodynamic clothing. The world record speed for the men's 1,000-meter event increased from 38 kilometers per hour in 1900 to 54 kilometers per hour in 2014. That's almost a 50 percent increase!

CHAPTER 8

CYCLING
OBREE
THE FLYING SCOTSMAN

Graeme Obree during his world hour record attempt,
in his tuck position, on his homemade bike

In the sport of cycling, the world hour record—how far you can cycle in exactly 60 minutes—is a big deal. And it's so tough that few riders ever try to break the record. Graeme Obree was an exception. He was going to have a shot. But in 1993, on a July afternoon in Hamar, Norway, only three people believed that Graeme Obree

49

could actually get the job done. Those three were Graeme, his wife, and his mother-in-law. Everyone else knew it was impossible. Why?

- Obree was a little-known amateur cyclist, not a famous professional like the other record-holders.

- The town of Hamar is at sea level. The previous records had been achieved at high altitudes, where thinner air allows you to cycle faster.

- Obree would be riding "Old Faithful" ... a bike he'd built himself ... at home. It even had a part taken from an old washing machine!

This was all challenging enough, but it wasn't the worst of it. The really bad news was that Obree had already tried—and failed. Earlier that afternoon, he'd fallen short of the record (more than 51 kilometers) by nearly half a kilometer.

A DIFFERENT ALARM CLOCK

Even though the odds were against him, Obree was still confident. The only thing that worried him was recovering from his failed attempt. Normally, it would take his body at least four days to bounce back from that effort. He had to sleep, but he knew that if he rested for more than a few hours, his muscles would stiffen up. He could set an alarm clock, but he didn't want a noisy, disturbing wake-up call. So he came up with another idea: before going to bed, he drank lots—and

lots—of water, and then let his bladder wake him up an hour or two later. He stretched for five or 10 minutes, ate a bowl of cornflakes to load his body with carbohydrates, drank a lot more water, and went back to sleep. After five or six cycles like this, he ate a final bowl of cornflakes at 8 a.m. and was on the track, ready to go, at nine.

As Obree got under way, his team did its best to urge him on. Every few laps, they held up cards to show Obree how he was doing against Francesco Moser's record of 51.151 kilometers, set in 1984. After 5 kilometers, Obree was a few thousandths of a second ahead. At 10 kilometers, his lead had stretched to 8 seconds. And he just kept going, increasing his lead with every 10 kilometers: 10 seconds, then 17 seconds, then 22 seconds by the 40-kilometer mark. Obree reached Moser's distance with 30 seconds to spare and smashed the record by nearly half a kilometer.

And they said it couldn't be done.

THE WORLD HOUR RECORD

Eddy Merckx, perhaps the most famous cyclist ever, set a world hour record of 49.431 kilometers in 1972. Merckx only attempted the record after he had won the Tour de France four years in a row. (The month-long race across France is like the Super Bowl of cycling.) After breaking the hour record, Merckx said, "[those 60 minutes] were the longest of my career ... I will never try it again." His record stood for 12 years before being broken by Francesco Moser, another cycling legend. Moser covered 51.151 kilometers.

Lubomír Vojta, a Czech cyclist who competes in both track and BMX events

Search for "Obree world hour record 1993" to find a video of Obree breaking the record.

51

WHY IT WORKS

What was Obree's advantage? How was he able to beat the odds and destroy Moser's record? Cycling at 50 kilometers an hour is a bit like perching on a stool in a 50-kilometer-per-hour wind. That's a very strong wind—not quite hurricane strong, but close. It takes effort to walk against such a gale, and it would certainly blow you right off your bike if you weren't prepared for it. If you want to stay on—and go faster for longer— you need to reduce your wind resistance. (At that speed, over 90 percent of your energy is used just to overcome that resistance.) Of course, the standard riding position was already pretty good at this. But Obree found a better position, giving him a small but significant edge. The new, improved position required a change to the bike, which is why Graeme built Old Faithful.

You'd think the cycling world would have applauded Obree's brilliant idea, and that other racers would have rushed to copy it in their own attempts to break records. You'd be wrong. Oh, sure, some people were intrigued. In fact, Francesco Moser didn't just copy Obree's technique (and bike), he added a chest bar to lean on. But that's pretty much where it stopped. Many cycling officials didn't like the "ugly" look of the tuck position. In April 1994, when Obree broke the record

This was the standard riding position. Note that the rider's arms make almost a right angle.

This is Obree's tuck position. The rider's arms are tucked in close to his body, like a downhill skier. To make this work, the handlebars need to be much higher than they are on a standard bike.

again, it seemed that the cheeky amateur had annoyed the officials too many times. The following month, the Union Cycliste Internationale (UCI)—the international committee that governs cycling—banned the tuck style.

Obree didn't take the ban lying down. He took it sitting up, with yet another new style. He found that by stretching his arms farther forward, keeping them less bent, he became even more streamlined. That position was nicknamed the "Superman," and lots of cyclists used it until 1996 when it, too, was banned by the grumpy UCI.

Obree's "Superman" position. The handlebars of the bike are modified to allow the rider's arms to stretch out.

DRAFTING

If you've ever watched a cycling race, you've probably noticed how riders often tuck in close to the bike in front of them. Now you can guess why. The rider in front shelters them from the wind. What a good deal: you save energy for later while the rider in front gets more and more tired. Actually, in long races, competitors will usually cooperate, and take turns being in front.

HOW TO MAKE YOUR BIKE GO FASTER

Banned or not, there's no question that Graeme Obree's innovations worked. They did so by stream-lining the rider. Others have worked at making the bike itself more efficient. Here are a few important technical innovations:

Streamlined helmets: Helmets are important for a very obvious reason. They protect your precious head if you crash! But the best helmets also serve another function. They are very light and are designed to be aerodynamic, cutting down on that wind resistance.

Disk wheels: A traditional bike wheel—the kind with lots of spokes—creates air turbulence. Air flows more smoothly over a disk, decreasing "drag." They're good, but riders need to be careful. While you can ride more quickly with disk wheels, a crosswind could also blow your bike over. The three large spokes pictured here are a compromise between traditional spoked wheels and disks. Using a disk only for the back (non-steering) wheel is often the best option.

Lighter bikes: Cyclists use muscle power to move the bike (and themselves). The lighter the bike, the faster and farther it can go. Racing bikes are now usually made of carbon fiber—as strong as steel but much lighter. However, the UCI won't allow too much efficiency: the rules state that bikes must weigh at least 6.8 kilograms.

HOW TO MAKE YOUR BIKE GO *EVEN FASTER*

People just weren't designed to be streamlined. A good way to overcome this sad fact is to build a streamlined shell, called a fairing, to go around the rider. This works really well—so well, in fact, that the UCI banned the use of fairings as long ago as 1914.

Another bright idea is to streamline the rider by having her lie down instead of sitting upright. Bicycles built for this type of riding are called "recumbent" (which means lying down) cycles. These can be either prone (face down) or supine (face up). Both forms work really well, and—you guessed it—the UCI banned them in 1934.

Fastest of all is to have a recumbent bike with a fairing. The UCI ban hasn't stopped people from building and racing these machines, called Human Powered Vehicles (HPVs). Just how efficient are they? The world hour record on UCI-approved bikes is just over 50 kilometers. The world hour record for an HPV, on the other hand, is over 90 kilometers. HPVs have reached speeds of over 130 kilometers an hour. That's faster than cars are allowed to drive on North American highways!

A recumbent bike with a fairing. Not built for serious racing, since the rider is still partly upright.

A serious racing recumbent bike without a fairing

Yup, there's a recumbent bike and rider inside that fairing.

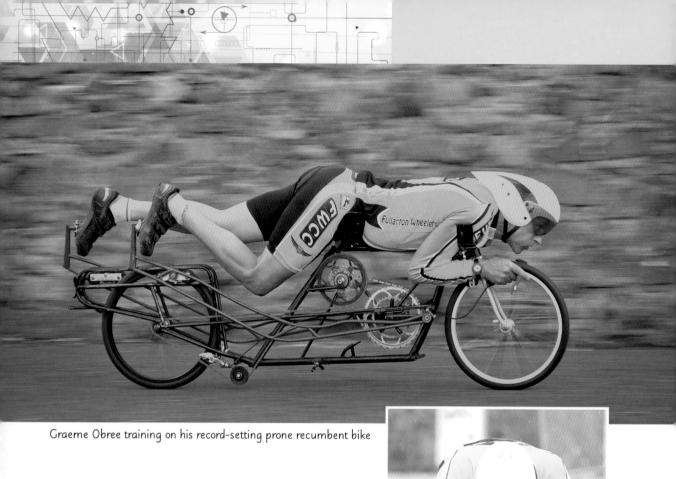

Graeme Obree training on his record-setting prone recumbent bike

STILL SPEEDING ALONG

In 2013, at the age of 48, Graeme Obree broke the world speed record for a prone recumbent bike (with no fairing). He clocked a speed of over 90 kilometers per hour.

It looks pretty uncomfortable, but it's clear how little wind resistance there is.

CHAPTER 9

WHEELCHAIR SPORTS HANG GLIDER TO WHEELER-DEALER

Before you jump off a mountain, there are a few things you have to do. Usually, Marilyn Hamilton did them all, and had a great time soaring in California's Sierra mountain range under her hang glider. But one day in 1978, she forgot to clip her harness to the glider. She was lucky not to be killed, but the crash broke her back. At the age of 29, Hamilton's life changed forever—but the lives of millions of others would also be changed by that simple mistake.

Hamilton was never able to walk again. After a stay in the hospital and three weeks of therapy, she was given a wheelchair and encouraged to get on with her life. She was eager to do that but worried about the things she would never be able to do again, like running, biking, squash and racquetball, hiking, and hang gliding.

Still, Hamilton was determined to live a full and active life, and ready to try new things. Regular tennis was out, but a friend got her started on wheelchair tennis. It was frustratingly difficult, and she'd come home from the courts at the end of the day with badly blistered hands. She hated her wheelchair! Its steel frame made it heavy (close to 27 kilograms, or 60 pounds) and hard to maneuver. And it was ugly. Being imprisoned in that wheelchair was the exact opposite of being able to fly in a hang glider. One day, that difference gave her an idea.

Hamilton talked to two friends who made hang gliders. She persuaded them to build her a new wheelchair using hang-glider technology. An aluminum frame made it strong but light; it was half the weight of her regular chair, and she could really move in it.

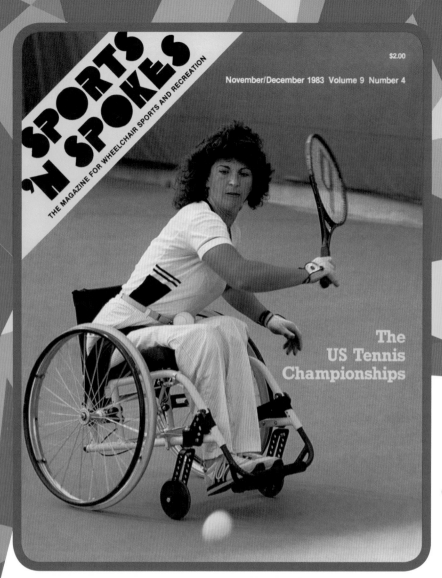

SPORTS 'N SPOKES
THE MAGAZINE FOR WHEELCHAIR SPORTS AND RECREATION

$2.00

November/December 1983 Volume 9 Number 4

The
US Tennis
Championships

Marilyn Hamilton excelled at tennis, winning the U.S. Open Women's Wheelchair Championship twice, in both singles and doubles. (Eventually she did get her yellow wheelchair.)

It even looked good. In fact, the only thing that stopped it from being absolutely perfect was that it was blue; she would have preferred yellow.

Hamilton and her friends knew they were on to something. Hamilton couldn't be the only one out there looking for a lighter, speedier chair. They formed a company to make and sell "Quickie" wheelchairs and specialized in meeting the needs of athletes. The company was hugely successful. Thirty-five years later, Quickie wheelchairs are still being bought by wheelchair athletes and others looking for a lighter-weight alternative to a traditional wheelchair—and Hamilton is still leading an active life!

WHEELCHAIR SPORTS

Wheelchair sports can be very competitive and very demanding. Elite wheelchair athletes have an awesome level of fitness, skill, and upper-body strength. Wheelchair basketball (upper picture) is very similar to stand-up basketball. Rules are adapted for wheelchairs. For example, only two pushes are allowed before a player must dribble the ball. Wheelchair rugby (lower picture) was developed by a group of Canadian athletes whose reduced arm and hand functions didn't allow them to compete equally in basketball. The objective is to carry the ball over the opponents' goal line.

Search for "wheelchair rugby" to see videos of this rough contact sport. You can see why it was first called murderball!

59

WHY THEY'RE BETTER

The reasons why a lightweight wheelchair is better for athletes than a traditional wheelchair are pretty easy to understand. In fact, Sir Isaac Newton figured out the exact math formulas to explain this stuff back in 1687, but here are the basics:

- **to move something heavy, you have to push harder;**

- **given the same push, something light will go faster than something heavy; and**

- **it's easier to slow down a lighter object than a heavier one.**

So, it's obvious that a lighter wheelchair will let an athlete move faster, stop faster, and change direction easily. The only thing that *isn't* obvious is why no one built a light wheelchair for athletes sooner. It seems this invention had to wait for Marilyn Hamilton: not only did she understand the need, she also had the connection to hang-gliding technology that turned a dream into a reality.

● Center of mass

A regular wheelchair tips over fairly easily. The vertical dotted black line shows that the center of mass is directly over the tipping point.

The wide wheelbase on a sports wheelchair makes it very stable and hard to tip over.

The lightness of the Quickie was the biggest innovation. But Hamilton and her friends didn't stop there. They worked hard to figure out what else an athlete would need. In the end, the Quickie was made more stable by giving it a lower center of mass and a wider wheelbase than a traditional wheelchair. An object will tip over when the center of mass is directly over the point of tipping. The diagram above shows that with a lower center of mass and a wider wheelbase, the sports wheelchair must be pushed to a much greater angle before it tips.

With a wheelchair, the center of mass is made lower by setting the seat lower. The Quickie also lets athletes adjust the height themselves. The wheelbase is made wider by using negative cambered wheels. This means that the wheels aren't vertical. Instead, they're angled so that the tops of the wheels are closer together than the bottoms.

——— Lever   ▲ Fulcrum   ⇒ Effort   ⇒ Output Force

Comparing a regular wheelchair and a cambered wheel: the cambered wheel on the left keeps the hand closer to the body. It forms a more efficient lever, delivering a harder push.

Another advantage of the negative cambered wheels is that the athlete can reach the wheel more easily. The top part of the wheel is close to the athlete's body, so the hands push almost in line with the athlete's shoulders and not out to the side. This lets you push harder. It's the same idea that was mentioned in the discussion of levers in Chapter 7. In this case, your upper arm is either a Class 2 or a Class 3 lever. The diagram shows how this works. The shoulder is the fulcrum, and the muscles in the upper arm provide the effort. The output force is delivered through the hand. The farther away your hand is from your shoulder when you push, the less output force you have.

TIPPING POINTS AND CENTER OF MASS

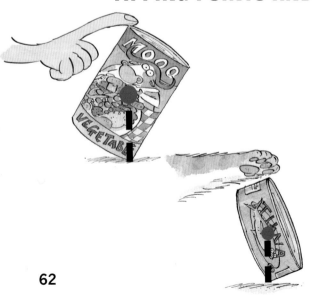

If you want to feel how the center of mass/tipping point principle works, grab a can of vegetables from the kitchen cupboard. Now mark the middle of the label with a dot. The center of mass is in the middle of the can, right behind that mark. With the mark facing you, hold the can on its edge just where it's balanced but about to tip over. Notice where the dot is? Right above the edge of the can. Now do the same thing with a shorter can, like the kind tuna comes in. There's no doubt which is more stable.

GUTTMANN'S GREAT IDEA

Dr. Ludwig Guttmann was a German brain surgeon who fled to England before the Second World War. During the war, he was in charge of Stoke Mandeville Hospital, a place that treated soldiers with spinal cord injuries. Before Guttmann, these patients were left to lie in bed, doing nothing. They would get painful bedsores, bladder and kidney infections, and would often die after several miserable months. No one expected them to become active again.

Guttmann refused to accept this. He believed he could use sport as a way to get patients active and out of bed. He got a sergeant assigned to the hospital to play catch with patients in bed, using a heavy medicine ball. (They needed to build up enough arm strength to lift themselves into a wheelchair.) Then the games really began. Activity wasn't optional; it was prescribed medicine. Patients had archery and darts, snooker and table tennis. They invented wheelchair polo and wheelchair basketball. As one patient put it, "We're so busy in this bloody place, we haven't got time to be ill." Amazingly, patients were soon being discharged from the hospital to go home and live active lives.

In 1948, Guttmann held the first annual wheelchair competition at the hospital. In 1952, Dutch competitors made these games international. Eight years later, they were held parallel to the Olympics. The Paralympics are now held immediately following the Olympics, in the same cities. In 1980, Guttmann watched 300 athletes enter Rome's Olympic stadium for the first Paralympic Games. That number's now increased to over 4,000 athletes. There are almost 600 different events in 27 sports, and there were 2.7 million spectators for the London 2012 games.

A racing wheelchair in action. Event distances range from 100 meters to the marathon (over 42 kilometers).

CHAPTER 10

SWIMMING THE BERKOFF BLASTOFF

David Berkoff was a pretty good backstroke swimmer—good enough to earn a spot on Harvard University's team. He wasn't setting world records or anything, but he was holding his own, at least until the day he discovered a secret: he could swim a heck of a lot faster if he started underwater, instead of on top. "I did a 15-meter kick out of the start, just to be a goof," Berkoff explained, "and I looked back and I saw that I had just smoked everyone." That one goofy start changed his life—and how the backstroke event played out in competition.

NEW TECHNIQUES, NEW RULES

Before his discovery, Berkoff had enjoyed racing well enough, but he wasn't so fond of training. Developing the underwater kick provided much-needed motivation. "Training became exciting because that was something new," he said. "The underwater portion made it fun."

He and his coach, Joe Bernal, worked hard to perfect the underwater start. There were days and weeks and months of kicking—dolphin and butterfly and backstroke—"a lot of trial and error," Berkoff said. They also went looking for some expert help. First up was the U.S. Coast Guard, which was studying submarines. Next came

David Berkoff at the 1998 Olympic Games

3-2-1 Blastoff!

65

the *real* experts: the porpoises at the Boston Aquarium. A visit to the facility proved that they sure knew how to kick underwater!

Three years later, all the hard work paid off. Berkoff was ready for the 1988 Olympics. He was able to swim 35 meters—most of the first length of the pool—underwater. Then he would pop up to the surface well ahead of everyone else. He broke the world record for the 100-meter backstroke twice during Olympic trials and again at the games in Seoul, South Korea. He won four medals at those games.

A pretty happy ending, except for one thing: right after those Olympic Games, the Fédération Internationale de Natation (FINA)—the committee that sets the rules for international swimming competitions—banned what had become known as the Berkoff Blastoff. They ruled that athletes could swim only the first 10 meters underwater. Eventually that rule was changed to allow 15 meters underwater.

Search for "1988 Olympics 100m backstroke" to find a video of the race. By the time of this race, most of the finalists are swimming long distances underwater.

BLASTOFF TECHNIQUE

Swimmers are ready, waiting for the starter's signal.

Swimmers kick off from the wall, reaching back as they enter the water.

Swimmers stay underwater for as long as possible, doing a dolphin kick. Berkoff stayed underwater for 35 meters. Now the rules only allow 15 meters.

WHY IT WORKS

Why does the Berkoff Blastoff provide swimmers with such an advantage? It's all about water resistance. As any object pushes through water, the water pushes back. This resistance is both a swimmer's best friend and worst enemy. Want to move forward? Push your hand or kick your foot backwards against the water and let the resistance—in this case, your best friend—push you forward. But the "worst enemy" part happens as soon as you start moving, when that same water resistance slows you down.

Swimmers experience the least resistance when they are streamlined, slicing through the water with their arms straight ahead and their body in a straight line. Of course, they still need to do something to move forward using their hands and/or feet.

It turns out that swimmers have more resistance on the surface than underneath. Moving along the surface, partly in water and partly in air, creates bubbles and waves, which slow you down. There's so much surface turbulence that swimming underwater using only a dolphin kick is faster than swimming on the surface using both hands and feet.

Not convinced? You can actually feel the best strategy for swimming fast by moving your hand through some water. Fill up your sink or bathtub.

First, push the water with your open palm. Lots of resistance, right? That's the way to propel your body forward.

Now turn your hand sideways and move it through the water again. That's how to get less resistance.

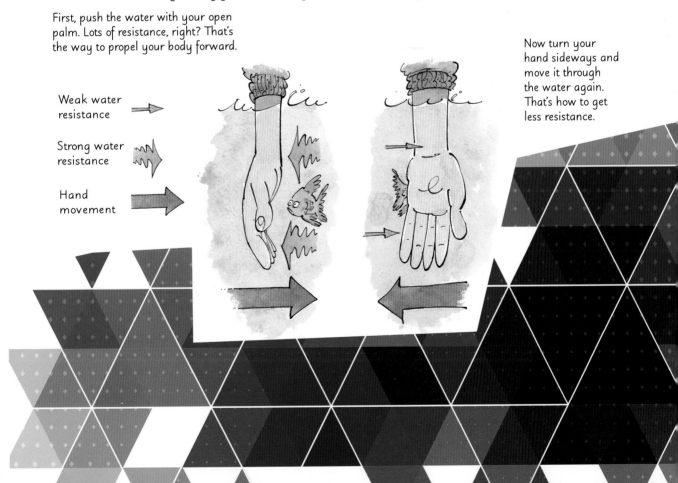

Weak water resistance

Strong water resistance

Hand movement

WHO GOT THERE FIRST?

Although the underwater trick is now known as the Berkoff Blastoff, others used the technique first. Although Berkoff broke the world record during heats, he only won the silver medal in the 100-meter final in Seoul; Japanese swimmer Daichi Suzuki edged him out to win gold. Four years earlier, at the 1984 Olympics, a 17-year-old Suzuki swam underwater for the first 25 meters of the 100-meter backstroke. Because he wasn't good enough then to make the finals, no one paid much attention.

Much earlier, at the 1956 Olympic Games in Melbourne, Australia, another Japanese swimmer, Masaru Furukawa, won the gold medal in the 200-meter breaststroke. Furukawa swam underwater for the first *three lengths* of the pool, coming up to breathe only at the turns. He then swam half the final length underwater as well, only swimming the last 25 meters at the surface. This caused a huge outcry, and underwater swimming was banned for breaststroke. These days, you're only allowed one kick underwater at the start of each length.

Search for "Hill Taylor 50m" to see just how fast underwater swimming really is. American Hill Taylor swims an entire 50-meter race underwater. He's disqualified—as he knew he would be—but he swims the race faster than the world record time.

WHY ALL THE BANNING?

The governing body of a sport has an important job: to make competition fair and uphold tradition. Part of this job means making sure that competition is based on the physical performance of the athlete and not on technology. Some high-tech swimsuits, which lowered racing times by 2 percent, have been banned for this reason.

Was banning underwater swimming the right move? When FINA banned the Berkoff Blastoff, they said it was for "safety concerns." Berkoff, for one, doesn't believe that. Did FINA think the technique changed the style too much? No one knows for sure. Watch some of the suggested videos and see what you think. Would you have banned underwater swimming?

HIGH-TECH SWIMSUITS

In 2010, FINA banned suits (like this one) made of buoyant polyurethane. And for men, suits can now only go from the waist to the top of the knees.

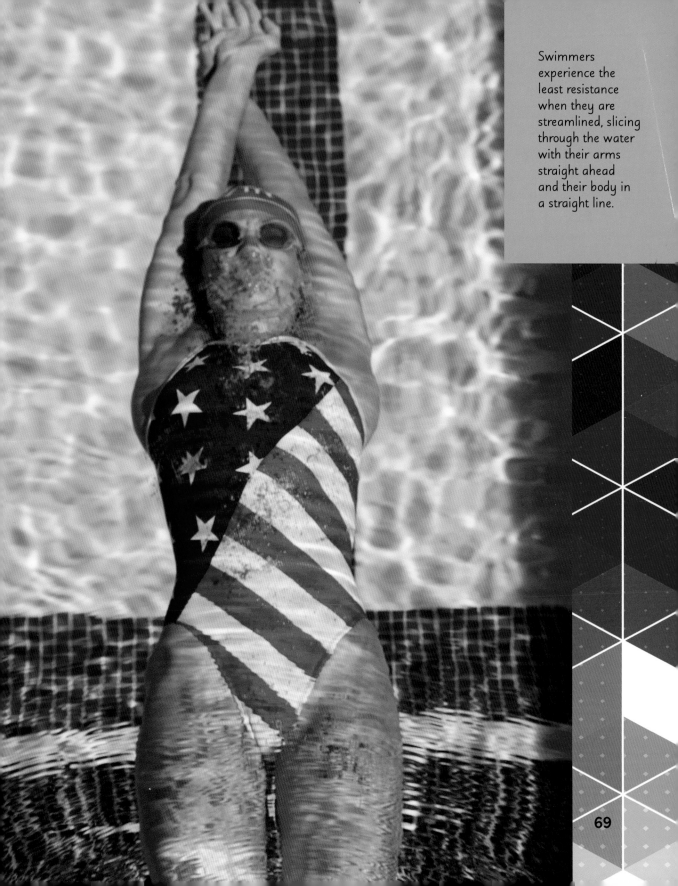

Swimmers experience the least resistance when they are streamlined, slicing through the water with their arms straight ahead and their body in a straight line.

69

CHAPTER 11

SKI JUMPING V FOR VICTORY

Ski jumping is a very weird sport! You ski down a ramp, reaching a speed of perhaps 90 kilometers an hour, and then you jump off the end. You float in the air down a mountain slope, looking a lot like a flying squirrel. You try not to fall down when you land. And you compete to see who can jump the farthest. (The world record is close to 250 meters—roughly the length of two and a half football fields.)

But none of that is the weird part. The weird part is that you get only about half your points for the distance you jump. The other half are awarded for "style," based on the opinion of five judges. So, if you want to succeed in ski jumping, the question is simple: what's considered good style?

THE GOOD, THE BAD, AND THE UGLY

In 1984, a 19-year-old Swedish ski jumper, Jan Boklöv, discovered something interesting. He wasn't great at the sport and was managing jumps of only 75 meters. But on one practice jump, his skis accidentally came apart into a V shape instead of remaining side by side in the traditional position. His groin muscles weren't strong enough to pull the skis back together, and so he sailed down the hill using the wrong jumping style. When he got to the bottom, he was shocked to see that this "bad style" had helped him land a 90-meter jump!

Jan Boklöv competing in a World Cup contest in Lahti, Finland, in 1989

Boklöv worked with his coach to further develop this untraditional approach. It wasn't easy—he broke his collarbone three times as he tried to perfect the technique—but within a few years, Boklöv was getting great distances on his jumps. Unfortunately, he still didn't do very well in competitions; he lost a lot of points for bad style. In fact, some people rudely called Boklöv's technique the "frog-style." Eventually, however, the rules changed and judges were only allowed to deduct a single point for the use of the V style. In 1989, Boklöv won five World Cup events and the overall championship.

Today, all ski jumpers use the V technique—and judges think it's *good* style!

PROFILE OF SKI JUMP HILL

INRUN

You build up speed in the inrun (the ramp). On TV, the inrun looks nearly vertical, but it's actually only about 35 degrees.

TABLE AND TAKEOFF

You jump as you reach the flat table at the end of the inrun. Timing your jump is difficult because things are happening very quickly: you cross the table in a quarter of a second! On TV, it looks as though the table slopes up. In fact, it slopes downward at about a 10-degree angle.

K-Point

LANDING HILL

You "fly" as far as possible over the convex landing hill (*convex* means it curves outward). The camera angles that most television networks use make it look as though the skiers are way up in the air, flying high. But this is an optical illusion. Depending on the hill, you're only 10 to 15 feet off the ground.

OUTRUN

The outrun is used to slow down and stop.

K-POINT

The K-Point is where the jumpers are "expected" to land. Judges will add points for landing farther, and subtract points for landing short of the K-Point.

The key to the V style's success is air resistance. During the inrun, you want to get as much speed as possible, so you want as little air resistance as possible. You tuck in, with your chest horizontal to your thighs and your arms straight back. If you've read Chapter 8: Cycling, this tucked position may look familiar: in both sports, cutting down on resistance is key.

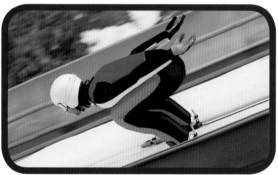

But during flight, everything changes. In fact, it's the exact opposite of the inrun. Now you lean forward and try to get as *much* air resistance as possible. Why? Because it's the air resistance that slows down your fall and allows you to glide farther.

Have a look at the diagrams below. With skis together and below the body (left), there's less surface area to create resistance. The skis shelter the body from the air. But when Boklöv accidentally slipped into the V position (right) during that practice run, he created more surface area for air resistance—both his body and his skis—and he jumped farther than he'd ever jumped before.

WHY DID THE RULES CHANGE?

The Fédération Internationale de Ski (FIS)—the governing body for international ski racing—does change rules from time to time. So why did they finally decide to accept the V style? No one knows for sure. Perhaps they just decided that being modern and forward-looking was a good thing, or that the V style really was better and should be allowed. In 2006, they made another bold move: they decided to allow women to ski jump at the 2009 World Championship! They went even further when they proposed to the International Olympic Committee (IOC) that women's ski jump be included in the 2010 Olympics. Sadly, the IOC was not as modern as the FIS. They rejected the proposal. Their reason? The five hundred women from 14 countries already competing internationally weren't enough to justify it as an Olympic sport. And apparently, they didn't think that making it an Olympic sport would be the best way to increase participation.

Anders Haugen

A LONG TIME TO WAIT

The sport of ski jumping is dominated by European countries. Only one American has ever won an Olympic medal for ski jumping. It happened in the first Winter Olympics, at Chamonix, France, in 1924. American Anders Haugen placed fourth, while the bronze medal went to Norway's Thorleif Haug, a superstar who had already won three gold medals at those games. But in 1974, at a Norwegian Olympic team reunion, a historian looked at the results and noticed that an error had been made. The scorer had incorrectly added the scores and given Haugen only 17.821 points, and not the 18.000 the judges had actually awarded. Correcting that mathematical mishap pushed Haugen into third place. At a special ceremony later that year, Haug's daughter presented Anders Haugen with his bronze medal—50 years after the competition!

Search for "ski jumping" to see videos of ski jumpers in action.

BEFORE BOKLÖV

Four years before Boklöv's accidental discovery of the power of V, another ski jumper competed successfully using an "upside-down V." Steve Collins was 15 years old, slim, and only 5 feet 3 inches tall. He was a Native Canadian from the Ojibwa tribe, living in a small town in Canada. He jumped with his skis in a V shape, but with the toes of the skis together rather than the heels. It's not quite as efficient as Boklöv's V, because the toes of the skis shelter some of the skier's body, cutting down on that all-important air resistance. Even so, using this style, Collins won the 1980 World Junior Championship, placed ninth in the Olympic Games, and won a World Cup jumping event, breaking the Finnish record for distance. Like Boklöv, Collins's success was limited because he lost lots of style points, even though his jumps were amazingly long.

Steve Collins competing at the 1980 Winter Olympics in Lake Placid.

CHAPTER 12

BLADE RUNNING
RUN LIKE A CHEETAH

Van Phillips

Van Phillips never wanted to be an inventor. His dream was to become a news broadcaster. But life had different plans. In 1976, when he was 22, he went waterskiing in Canyon Lake, Arizona, with his girlfriend and his college roommate. Phillips had just gotten up on a slalom ski and taken a big cut to the left when his roommate's boat caught fire. As another boat came around a rocky outcrop, its driver swerved to avoid the scene. He didn't see Phillips in the water. The boat hit Phillips, and its propeller cut off his foot. He woke up in the hospital the next morning to find only a stump below the knee. His life was changed, but Phillips wasn't about to let it be wrecked.

A few weeks later, he was fitted with a prosthesis (an artificial limb), taught to walk on it, and told he was good to go. And he was—at least when it came to walking short distances on a smooth floor. But for Phillips, this was nowhere near good enough. He wanted to go hiking in the wilderness; he wanted to go to the beach and surf; he wanted to play tennis; he wanted to run! The prosthesis was made of wood, so it was heavy. Hiking with it would probably have been about as miserable as if you had to hike with a 1.5-kilogram weight (like a bag of sugar) attached to your ankle. Speaking of the ankle, that was a problem too: it didn't bend, so there was no give as the foot came down, making it very hard to run. And the way the whole prosthesis fit the stump made it about as comfortable as walking around with a sharp pebble in your shoe.

Phillips did some research. He learned that there hadn't really been any improvements in prostheses for 30 years. Companies hadn't invested money to improve them, mostly because there weren't enough customers to make a big profit. Phillips realized that he couldn't wait for others to make a good prosthesis. If he really wanted one, he would have to build it himself.

INFAMOUS OSCAR

Oscar "Blade Runner" Pistorius. You've likely heard the name. This South African double-amputee is the most famous, and most infamous, athlete to use the Flex-Foot Cheetah blades. He was the first double-amputee to compete in the Olympic Games. In the 2012 Olympics, held in London, he reached the final of the 4 x 100-meter relay, and the semifinal of the 400-meter race. But perhaps even more newsworthy was what happened two years later: Pistorius was charged with the murder of his girlfriend, Reeva Steenkamp. He was not convicted of murder, but the courts did find him guilty of "culpable homicide" (similar to manslaughter).

Search for "2012 Olympics 400m Pistorius" for videos of the first double-amputee running in the Olympic Games.

The huge C-shaped tendon in the hind leg of the cheetah inspired the design.

BUILDING THE BLADE

Phillips transferred out of journalism and enrolled in one of the best programs in America for prosthetic design. After graduating, he went to work at the Center for Biomedical Design at the University of Utah, which was famous for developing an artificial arm. The whole time, he was thinking about how to design a foot that would let him run. Phillips had been a pole-vaulter in high school, and he remembered the feeling of how the flexible pole stored and then released energy. He wanted that kind of flexing for his foot. But how could he get it?

For years, Phillips thought about what the right shape for his new foot might be. His inspiration was the hind leg of a cheetah, the fastest animal in the world. It has a hugely powerful, C-shaped tendon. At each stride, the tendon stretches and then releases that energy. Phillips looked at many different materials before deciding that carbon

fiber—light, strong, and flexible—would be a good choice.

At last, he started building prototype feet. After 10 not-so-great attempts (they all broke!), Phillips met Dale Abildskov, an aerospace engineer who was an expert in carbon fiber. In only three weeks, Abildskov and Phillips built a foot that allowed Phillips to sprint down the corridor outside his office. Phillips's patience had finally paid off.

In 1983, Phillips and Abildskov started Flex-Foot, a company that makes and sells prosthetic feet especially for athletes. Phillips's original design is still sold as the Flex-Foot Cheetah, and it's still the first choice for most runners. Flex-Foot has also designed specialized feet for other activities, including swimming, skiing, and mountain climbing. Athletes with Flex-Foot feet have competed in the Olympic Games and climbed to the top of Mount Everest.

As the foot comes down, the blade is compressed, turning kinetic (motion) energy into elastic energy. At the end of the stride, the blade comes back to its original shape, turning that elastic energy back into kinetic energy, pushing the runner forward. The blades are very efficient, returning 90 percent of the energy that goes into compressing them. The soles of the feet have spikes to help grip the track, just like the spikes on the soles of regular running shoes.

Although the design looks simple, a lot goes into it. For example, the toe has fewer layers of carbon fiber, to make it more flexible, while the upper portion has more layers, to handle higher stress forces. The overall shape of the foot, without a heel, allows an efficient movement.

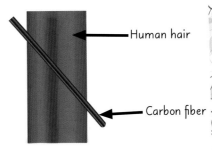

Human hair

Carbon fiber

CARBON FIBER

Carbon fiber is much thinner than a human hair (compare sizes in the picture above). It's a very strong filament made mostly of carbon atoms, linked to form chains. The filament is woven into fabric and then "glued" with resin to form sheets. The sheets, in turn, are layered to form very light, strong materials.

Kinetic (motion) energy is turned into elastic energy, compressing the blade.

The blade recovers, turning elastic back into kinetic energy.

IS IT FAIR?

Is it fair to non-amputee athletes to allow amputee athletes to compete against them? Do these blades give an unfair advantage? Olympic committees had to answer this question when Oscar Pistorius wanted to compete for the South African team. A group of scientists decided he did not have an unfair advantage, but the question continues to be debated. Using blades has both advantages and disadvantages. An amputee runner doesn't have calf and foot muscles to generate power. On the other hand, blades are roughly half the weight of legs, so the amputee can move them more quickly and uses less energy to run. Pistorius was known for starting more slowly than his competitors, and then running the second 200 meters faster than the first—unheard of for a non-amputee athlete.

OLYMPIC ACHIEVEMENTS

Oscar Pistorius may have been the first *double*-amputee to compete in the Olympics, but a number of single-amputees have competed. Amazingly, back in 1904 in St. Louis, Missouri, an American amputee won three gold medals in gymnastics. George Eyser placed first in vault, parallel bars, and rope climbing—all with a wooden leg! For good measure, he also won two more silvers and a bronze.

AMAZING AMPUTEES

Many amputees show amazing courage and determination. Here are just two:

Aimee Mullins was born without fibulae (the bones in the lower leg). Using Phillips's Cheetah foot, she was the first amputee to compete in the National Collegiate Athletic Association (NCAA) in the U.S., and she set world records for double-amputees in the 100-meter, 200-meter, and long jump events. She led the U.S. delegation to the 2012 London Olympics—the biggest honor that the U.S. Olympic Committee can give. Mullins says that being an amputee doesn't mean she is *disabled*—it means she has *options*. She has 12 pairs of legs, and she enjoys choosing what height she wants to be—anything from 5 feet 8 inches to 6 feet 1 inch.

Tom Whittaker's right leg had to be amputated after a bad automobile accident. He got a specially designed Flex-Foot with ice crampons (sharp studs) and, on his third try, he reached the top of Mount Everest—the highest mountain in the world. He now wants to be the first amputee to climb the peak of the highest mountain on each of the seven continents.

Aimee Mullins

Tom Whittaker

81

CHAPTER 13

SKIING AND TENNIS
A HEAD FOR INNOVATION

Howard Head was a good aeronautical engineer. He was not a natural athlete. That turned out to be a very good thing for two sports.

SKIING

In the spring of 1947, at the age of 32, Howard Head decided to try skiing. On the ski slopes of Vermont, he discovered that he *loved* skiing; he also discovered that he was pretty terrible at it. He was willing to admit that lack of talent might be part of the problem, but he also believed that the skis were no good. In Head's opinion, the wooden skis that were popular at the time were too heavy and clumsy. He figured he could make better ones. He was using honeycombed plastic sandwiched between sheets of aluminum to make airplane fuselages. He would use the same technology to make strong, light skis.

At Christmas that year, Head took six prototype lightweight skis back to Vermont for a trial. Ski instructors tested them just by flexing the skis. Five of the six pairs broke immediately. Head skied on the sixth pair for about 20 minutes before those broke too. Most people would have given up. Instead, Head quit his job at the Glenn L. Martin aircraft company so that he could work full-time on building a better ski. It took four years, but finally he got it done—and the skis were brilliant. They were so much easier for beginners that they were nicknamed "cheaters." Even though they were very expensive, Head skis became the bestselling skis in the world. In the 1960s, half of all skis in the U.S. were Heads.

WHY THEY WORK

Head's first idea of making the skis much lighter was not the right one. Light skis turned out to be unstable at higher speeds. He eventually used layers of aluminum, plywood, and plastic, with steel edges. Three things made Head skis so good:

Plastic —
Steel —
Plastic —
— Aluminum
— Plywood
— Aluminum

- ● **They were very flexible along the length and could easily bend anywhere from front to back.**

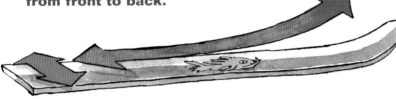

- ● **They were very stiff *torsionally*, meaning that they didn't bend or twist easily from side to side.**

  - ● **The steel edges were sharp.**

The combination of these characteristics made it easy for a skier to turn. The flexible skis could bend to fit the curve of the turn, and the torsional stiffness and steel edges allowed the skis to cut through snow (or even ice) to hold the edge without skidding.

Head skis being used in an international competition

TENNIS

At the age of 55, Howard Head sold his ski company, retired, and tried playing tennis. He discovered that he *loved* tennis; he also discovered that he was pretty terrible at it. He was willing to admit that lack of talent might be part of the problem, but he also believed the racket was no good. In Head's opinion, the wooden rackets that were popular at the time were too heavy and too small. Once again, he took matters into his own hands.

Head was so bad at tennis that his teacher refused to work with him unless he promised to practice every day. Head bought a machine that hit balls to him so he could keep that promise. Then he took the machine apart to see how it worked. He wasn't very impressed. He bought the company (called Prince) that made it and redesigned the machine. It became the bestselling ball machine in the world. Then he started working on a better racket for his new company to sell.

Head built a racket with a face 30 percent bigger than regular rackets. He used aluminum instead of wood, for both strength and lightness. Players saw the new rackets and said, "They must be illegal." They weren't. There were absolutely no rules specifying what size tennis rackets could be, or what materials could be used to make them. Like Head's skis had been years before, Head's rackets were much easier to use, especially for beginners and intermediate players. Within four years, one out of every four tennis rackets sold around the world was a Prince racket.

Head's rackets (right) had faces that were 30 percent bigger than regular rackets.

HOW IT WORKS

Head's tennis rackets have three things going for them: twist resistance, the location of the "sweet spot," and swing speed.

TWIST RESISTANCE

If you don't hit the ball exactly on the center axis of a racket, the racket will twist and the ball will bounce off at an angle. It won't go exactly where you want it to go.

Doing! Doing! Doing!

The ball meets the racket on the center axis. The racket doesn't twist, and the ball goes back in the direction that the racket is swinging.

1

1. The ball meets the racket off to the side of the center axis, and the impact of the ball causes the racket to twist.
2. The ball is deflected in the direction that the racket has twisted.

2

Clunk!

Because Head's racket is wider, it doesn't twist as easily, which means that a ball hit off center won't go as far off course. That could make the difference between hitting the net or clearing it. The measurement of how easily something will twist is called its "moment of inertia." Read the sidebar on page 88 for more on moment of inertia.

A MOVING SPOT

That sweet spot is a tricky thing. Not only does it sit lower on the racket than you might expect, but it's also a moving target! The position of the sweet spot depends on the speed of the racket. During a serve, the racket is moving faster and the sweet spot is higher up the racket. For regular ground shots, the racket speed is slower, so the sweet spot shifts down.

The sweet spot on Head's new racket was closer to the center. That makes it easier to connect the ball and the spot.

THE "SWEET SPOT"

When you whack a tennis ball just right, you can tell. Your swing feels smooth and effortless; the ball makes a satisfying sound as it connects with the racket, and the ball really takes off. That's what happens when you hit the racket's sweet spot. The sweet spot—or "power spot," as it's sometimes called—is the point on the racket where there is the most bounce. And that's where you need to hit the ball to get the most speed. It would be nice and simple if the sweet spot were in the middle of the racket face, but it isn't; it's actually much lower. Head's new racket helped players connect because the sweet spot is closer to the center of the bigger face.

● The sweet spot

SWING SPEED

Head's aluminum racket was lighter than the old wooden ones. That meant you could swing it faster. Hitting the ball with a faster weapon means the ball goes faster. (See Chapter 3: Baseball for more on how this works.)

A BALANCING ACT

You might have noticed something that seems wrong. Head's racket is better because it's lighter and therefore faster. It also has a greater moment of inertia, because it's wider. But doesn't the fact that it's lighter mean that it has a *smaller* moment of inertia? Yes, that's right. It's like adding a positive and a negative number together. Head designed it so that the combination of the two still gave the racket a greater moment of inertia than the traditional rackets.

Serena Williams in action at the 2013 U.S. Open. When you're as good as she is, you have no trouble hitting the sweet spot.

STRING THEORY

You would think that to hit the ball hard, the strings on your racket should be tight. Wrong! In fact, looser strings hit the ball harder. They work like a trampoline, turning the ball's kinetic energy (energy of motion) into elastic energy (stored by stretching the strings). The strings then return that elastic energy into kinetic energy, sending the ball on its way faster. When the strings are tighter, they cause the ball to deform. That turns kinetic energy into heat and sound energy, which is not returned to the ball. It's the same thing that happens when a baseball meets an aluminum bat (see Chapter 3: Baseball).

Loose strings are like a trampoline!

87

MOMENT OF INERTIA

This is a measure of how much effort is needed to twist (or spin) an object. The higher the moment of inertia, the more effort is needed to create a twist. Two things determine an object's moment of inertia: its mass (weight) and its shape. The more mass it has, the bigger its moment of inertia. And the farther that parts of the object are from the axis, the bigger is its moment of inertia. Skaters doing a spin understand this really well.

Skaters make their routines interesting by using different positions to vary the look and the speed of a spin. The camel spin, with the body and one leg held horizontal to the ice, makes for a big moment of inertia, and a slow spin. The Biellmann spin is named after its inventor, Switzerland's Denise Biellmann. With her free leg, arms, and trunk close to the axis of rotation, she had a small moment of inertia, making for a very fast spin.

2011 U.S. national champion Ryan Bradley doing a camel spin

Axis of rotation

You start spinning with your arms out wide. Pulling them into your body decreases your moment of inertia. Spinning becomes easier, so you spin much faster.

Tightrope walkers also know all about moments of inertia: to increase their moment of inertia—which makes them more stable on the rope and decreases their chances of falling—they use long poles like the one pictured below.

S. J. DIXON CROSSING NIAGARA ON 7/8 INCH WIRE
453-14

Samuel Dixon uses the long rod's moment of inertia to help maintain balance as he crosses the Niagara River (1890).

Elene Gedevanishvili has represented Georgia (the country, not the U.S. state) at three Olympic Games. Here she's doing a Biellmann spin.

Search for "Biellmann spin" to see a video of Denise Biellmann's trademark move. It's a great demonstration of the effect that a changing moment of inertia can have.

CHAPTER 14

BUNGY JUMPING
A LEAP OF FAITH

On the night of June 25, 1987, A. J. Hackett was so comfortable in his sleeping bag that he overslept by half an hour. Most people wouldn't be so relaxed, hiding illegally 110 meters (360 feet) off the ground on the second level of the Eiffel Tower. But then again, most people wouldn't have scoped out the security on the tower—making note of gates, fences, locks, and cameras, and timing the guards' routine. Most people also wouldn't have planned how to block security cameras using umbrellas and cardboard, how to distract the guards with a couple of attractive women, or how to sneak over a fence and out of sight in a maintenance area. Oh, and most people wouldn't have wanted to jump off the tower at dawn. But A. J. Hackett isn't most people.

Hackett had come to France as a member of the New Zealand speed skiing team. After the competition, he hung around looking for excitement until he ran out of money. That lack of cash triggered a crazy idea: he partnered with a video company to photograph him jumping off the tower, and they planned to split the money from selling the pictures worldwide.

Waking up half an hour late meant the team had to rush from its hiding spot to the jump point. Hackett started one final check of the height by lowering a small weight

A. J. Hackett about to jump off the Eiffel Tower

on a fishing line. Suddenly, they heard a steady *clang, clang, clang*—footsteps coming up a nearby stairwell. It was still half dark. Security guards weren't due for at least an hour—not until the elevators started running. Was the team busted? The footsteps came closer and then continued up the stairs. It was staff from the café on the level above them, on their daily hike to work.

Hackett fastened one end of his rubber bungy (pronounced bun-jee) cord to the tower and the other end to his ankles. Peering over the side, he noticed a bunch of backpackers camped out below the tower in the jump area, fast asleep. Hackett's team below woke them and moved them out of the way.

Search for "A. J. Hackett Eiffel Tower" **to see footage of the famous jump.**

That attracted the attention of police, and a little squad gathered to watch. It was time.

Wearing a tuxedo—after all, it's not every day you hope to be front-page news around the world—Hackett jumped. It went perfectly. He didn't hit the ground, but he came close. He bounced up and down a few times before being lowered gently to the ground. The police arrested him, but they didn't know what to do next. There weren't any laws saying you're not allowed to jump off the Eiffel Tower—no one had thought one was needed! So when Hackett showed them his passport and a plane ticket proving he was about to go back to New Zealand, they let him go.

Best of all, there were no big news stories that day, so the video of Hackett's jump off the Eiffel Tower was shown around the world. Bungy Jumping became instantly famous, and Hackett along with it. He used that fame to start a number of Bungy-Jumping businesses around the world.

If you jump off the Eiffel Tower, expect to be arrested by the French police.

91

When you are standing on a high platform, you have potential energy. The higher you are, the more potential energy you have.

HOW IT WORKS

Since that Eiffel Tower jump, millions of people have paid money to leap off towers and bridges—many of them much higher than that famous jump. But how does Bungy Jumping work?

When you leap off a high building or a bridge with a bungy cord attached to you, you set in motion a battle between gravity (pulling downward) and the elastic bungy cord (pulling upward). Gravity always pulls with a constant force, but the cord only starts pulling when it's stretched—and the more it's stretched, the harder it pulls. The diagram helps to explain.

After you jump, gravity starts to convert that potential energy into kinetic (motion) energy. As gravity continues to pull you down, you *accelerate* (you fall faster and faster).

As the cord starts stretching, it begins to pull you upward. Gravity pulls harder than the bungy, so you still accelerate downward, but you accelerate more slowly. The pull of the stretching cord converts your kinetic energy into elastic energy within the cord.

The more the cord stretches, the harder it pulls. Eventually the pull of the cord gets to be stronger than gravity. You still keep falling, but now you *decelerate* (you fall more slowly). Your kinetic energy continues to be converted to elastic energy.

Unstretched cord length

Gravity stronger than pull of cord

Pull of cord stronger than gravity

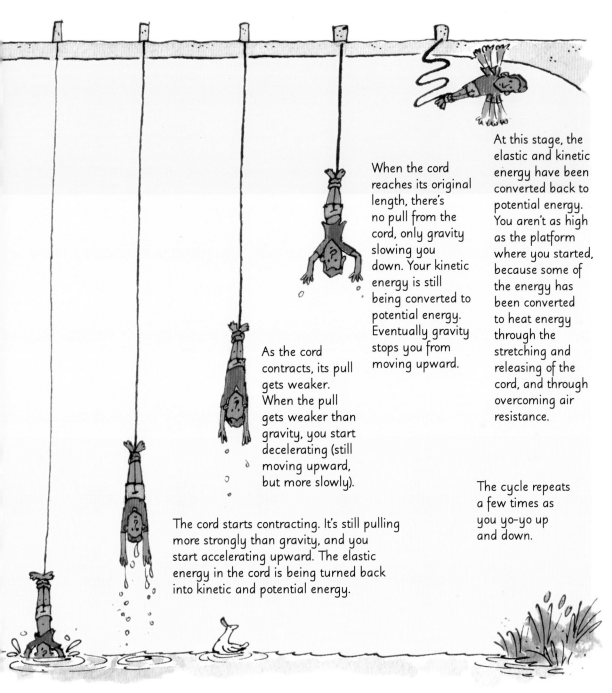

When the cord reaches its original length, there's no pull from the cord, only gravity slowing you down. Your kinetic energy is still being converted to potential energy. Eventually gravity stops you from moving upward.

At this stage, the elastic and kinetic energy have been converted back to potential energy. You aren't as high as the platform where you started, because some of the energy has been converted to heat energy through the stretching and releasing of the cord, and through overcoming air resistance.

As the cord contracts, its pull gets weaker. When the pull gets weaker than gravity, you start decelerating (still moving upward, but more slowly).

The cord starts contracting. It's still pulling more strongly than gravity, and you start accelerating upward. The elastic energy in the cord is being turned back into kinetic and potential energy.

The cycle repeats a few times as you yo-yo up and down.

For an instant, you come to a stop. If all has gone right, at this stage, you'll be just above the water (or ground). Or perhaps just under water. Yikes!

93

THE IMPORTANCE OF ELASTICITY

Now that you know how Bungy Jumping works, you can also imagine how important it is to have the right cord for the job. The bungy cord is made of 20 to 30 strands of latex rubber, each about as thick as the lead in a pencil. The strands are then wrapped with diagonal strips of latex rubber. (Latex rubber is made by processing liquid from under the bark of rubber trees.)

The most important decision for a jump is how long and how thick a cord to use. The choice depends on the height of the platform and the weight of the jumper. A heavier jumper will stretch the cord more than a lighter one. It's crucial that the cord stretches enough to slow you down gradually. You don't want it to jerk you to a very quick stop. And you absolutely don't want it to break! A strand of rubber will stretch to almost seven times its length before breaking. When Hackett perfected his technique, his goal was to stretch the cord to about four times its length. That's a good safety margin.

Robert Hooke, a British physicist, discovered the basic laws of elasticity in 1660. You can use his laws to figure out how long and thick to make the bungy cord. It turns out, for example, that doubling the weight of a jumper will double the length of the cord's stretch. Doubling the thickness of the cord will halve the length of the stretch.

Safety in numbers! A bungy cord is made up of lots of thin rubber strands.

Bungy Jumping from the Kawarau Bridge in Queenstown, New Zealand. This was the world's first commercially operated Bungy Jump.

STAYING SAFE

When A. J. Hackett took his famous leap off the Eiffel Tower, he knew exactly what he was doing. He'd spent months learning about cord and jump safety. Choosing the length and thickness of the cord was important, but Hackett knew there was more to it than that. Here are just a few of the ways that good Bungy Jump operators help keep you safe.

- **Cord checks: Cords deteriorate with use. A safety-conscious operator will trash them after 300 or 400 jumps, although they would actually be good for a few thousand more jumps.**

- **Safety procedures: There's no room for carelessness; the operator of a jump needs to have a procedure for double-checking that the cord is securely attached to you and to the platform.**

- **Training: The "jump master" is critically important. Hackett's operations require someone to have years of experience before being allowed to be in charge of a jump.**

A. J. Hackett is proud that his operations have jumped more than 3.5 million people, and none have died. But people have died in jumps operated by others. If you're ever adventurous enough to go Bungy Jumping, choose the operator carefully.

95

SPEED SKIING

The extreme sport of speed skiing—one of Hackett's early activities—is at least as terrifying as Bungy Jumping. The first half of the 1-kilometer course is very steep, pretty much straight down a mountain. You ski down as fast as possible. Your speed is measured over a 100-meter stretch near the bottom. Then you use the rest of the course to stop. World record speeds are over 250 kilometers an hour. That's more than double the speed limit on any highway in North America!

Speed skiing looks pretty similar to the inrun portion of ski jumping—but is much longer. Check out the neat aerodynamic clothing and space-age helmet. The weird-looking fins behind the calves are designed to decrease drag in the tuck position.

WHERE IT ALL STARTED

The inspiration for Bungy Jumping came from a ritual in the Pentecost Island of Vanuatu, 1,600 kilometers (1,000 miles) northwest of Australia. Once a year, the men of the island build a wooden tower. They carefully choose vines that they fasten to the tower and tie around their ankles. Then they dive off the tower! There is only ground below; they rely solely on the vines to prevent them from smashing into the ground. By comparison, Bungy Jumping is tame.

The custom is based on a legend: A man called Tamalie repeatedly mistreated his wife. One day, she ran away from him and climbed a tree. From the top of the tree, his wife laughed at him and called him a coward. He followed her up the tree. When he reached the top, she jumped. He jumped after her. But she had tied vines to her ankles, so she survived. He did not. The annual "land diving" festival celebrates her cleverness and bravery.

A Pentecost Island
ritual: the inspiration
for Bungy Jumping

CHAPTER 15

CHEATING STEROID SCANDALS

The end of the Seoul Olympics' 100-meter race.
For Ben Johnson, this was the end in more ways than one.

Search for "1988 Olympics 100m" to see videos of the famous Lewis–Johnson race.

The seventy thousand fans crammed into the stadium in Seoul, South Korea, are just a drop in the bucket. On the other side of the world, tens of millions of North Americans are glued to their television sets, ready to watch the biggest grudge match of the 1988 Olympics—the 100-meter

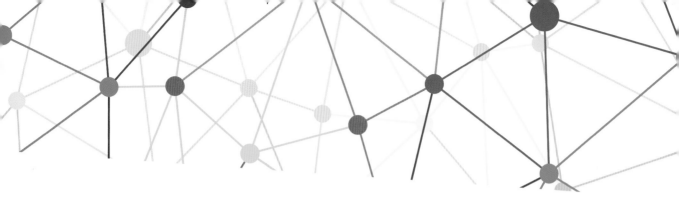

final. The favorites? American Carl Lewis and Canadian Ben Johnson, both of whom desperately want to win. The race is too close to call. Lewis captured the Olympic gold medal in 1984, while Johnson took the bronze. In 1987, Johnson snatched the world record away from Lewis with a time of 9.83 seconds. And just a month ago, racing in Zurich, Lewis crossed the finish line first. Which sprinter is going to take this contest? Johnson has a faster start, but Lewis was speedier in the qualifying heats. "King Carl" is more graceful, "Big Ben" more muscular. The tension is high. Before the race, the two men stalk around the starting area like menacing big cats. It's no secret that these guys hate each other.

When the gun finally goes off, Johnson reacts first. After 10 meters, he's 6/100ths of a second ahead of Lewis. At 20 meters, 9/100ths. At 40 meters, 12/100ths. By the 60-meter mark, Johnson is a full 2 meters ahead of the pack. At 80 meters, he starts relaxing a little. With 5 meters to go, he looks over at Lewis and raises an arm in victory. He stops the clock at 9.79 seconds—a new world record! Big Ben has dethroned King Carl, who finishes second with a personal best time of 9.92 (and is pretty much ignored when he tries to shake Johnson's hand). An ocean away, Canada goes crazy celebrating. The prime minister even calls Johnson to offer his congratulations. There's no doubt about it: this race will be remembered forever.

A RACE TO REMEMBER

Unfortunately, the Seoul Olympics' dramatic 100-meter final is remembered for more than just amazing sprinting. Yes, it was the first time four runners broke the 10-second mark in the same race, but that's not why it has a permanent place in the history books. Three days after the race, it was revealed that Johnson's urine had tested positive for a banned drug—an anabolic steroid. Johnson was stripped of his gold medal, which went to Lewis. At first, Johnson claimed that he'd been wrongly accused. Later, though, he admitted that he'd been taking steroids for years. Not long after, his 1987 record was removed from the record books. Another Canadian Olympic athlete, swimmer Mark Tewksbury,

summed up the sad situation when he was quoted as saying that Johnson went from "hero to zero in 9.79 seconds."

JOHNSON'S NOT ALONE

Like Johnson, many other famous athletes have been celebrated as heroes before being revealed as cheaters who relied on performance-enhancing drugs.

CYCLING

In 2005, American Lance Armstrong was arguably the best cyclist ever. That year, he won the Tour de France—the most prestigious cycling event in the world—for the seventh time in a row. A few years later, however, he admitted the rumors that had been dogging him for years were true: he *had* been using banned performance-enhancing drugs (PEDs). All of his Tour de France wins were scrubbed from the record books and he was banned for life from racing.

Armstrong in 2009. He returned to racing that year after having retired in 2005.

BASEBALL

By the early 2000s, steroid use in baseball had become so common that an investigation into the problem was launched. The resulting report listed players believed to have used PEDs, including batting greats José Canseco and Mark McGwire.

TRACK AND FIELD

In 2007, American track and field star Marion Jones admitted to using steroids—but only after denying the charges for years, including in front of two juries investigating steroid use in sport. When she finally did come clean, she was stripped of five Olympic medals and sentenced to six months in prison.

NOT ALL INNOVATIONS ARE GOOD

When it comes to sports, the use of anabolic steroids is definitely not an innovation to celebrate. Anabolic steroids are a manufactured substance very similar to testosterone—a hormone that occurs naturally in the body. You may have heard testosterone called the "male hormone"; that's because males produce about 20 times as much as females. Testosterone promotes the development of muscle, and so its artificial form is useful in treating patients with some diseases, including cancer. Even so, doctors use anabolic steroids carefully and sparingly, because the side effects can be serious.

Dr. John Ziegler was the so-called godfather of anabolic steroids. Ziegler was a medical doctor, a part-time pharmaceutical researcher at Ciba Pharmaceuticals, and an amateur weight lifter. In 1964, he went to the World Weightlifting Championships in Austria as the doctor to the U.S. team. The Russians won handily. Ziegler sat down for a chat with his Russian counterpart, who told him that the Russian team was being given testosterone. It was working well, except for some bad side effects. For example, one young weight lifter was no longer able to pee normally; they'd had to insert a catheter (a thin tube) to drain his bladder.

Ziegler went home and started searching for a drug that would build muscle like testosterone, but without the side effects. Through his work at Ciba, he identified an anabolic steroid called Dianabol. After he tested it on himself and noticed only limited side effects, he gave it to a number of competitive weight lifters. It worked to increase their strength, and the use of the drug spread, with some athletes taking many times the recommended dose. Not surprisingly, the side effects spread too.

Ziegler died of heart failure in 1983. He blamed his illness at least partly on his steroid use. Shortly before his death, he said, "I wish to God now I'd never done it. I'd like to go back and take that whole chapter out of my life."

WHY TAKING STEROIDS ISN'T A SMART MOVE

There are at least three very good reasons not to take steroids to improve performance:

- ⦿ **It's illegal.**
- ⦿ **It's cheating.**
- ⦿ **It has nasty side effects.**

facial hair

male-pattern baldness
severe acne

deep voice

heart disease

smaller breasts

enlarged breasts

liver cancer
kidney damage

infertility

smaller testicles

stunted growth

OTHER WAYS TO CHEAT

Using steroids and other performance-enhancing drugs is the most common way of cheating. But athletes have found other ways to demonstrate their dishonesty to the world.

At the 1976 Olympics in Montreal, Soviet athlete **BORIS ONISCHENKO** was expected to win a medal in the modern pentathlon. Fencing, one of the five sports in pentathlon, uses electronic scoring. When an épée (sword) touches an opponent's strike zone, the scoreboard automatically shows a point scored. But during matches with British opponents, the scoreboard lit up even when Onischenko clearly missed. The épée was taken away and examined. It had been tampered with—and was designed to register a hit whenever a button was pushed. Onischenko was disqualified and sent home in disgrace. Today, he's remembered by the nickname that newspapers quickly gave him: "Disonischenko."

In 1980, **ROSIE RUIZ** won the Boston Marathon in a record time. Officials were immediately suspicious. Ruiz was an unknown runner and wasn't really tired or even sweaty. She couldn't describe aspects of the course, and no one could remember seeing her until just before the end of the race. An investigation proved that she had run out of a crowd of spectators and onto the course half a mile before the finish line. A week later, she was stripped of the title.

Ruiz wasn't the first cheater to "win" a prominent marathon. During the 1904 St. Louis Olympics, American **FRED LORZ** crossed the finish line first. After cheers from the crowd, and being crowned with a laurel wreath, Lorz admitted the truth. He had dropped out of the race with cramps, ridden about 18 kilometers (11 miles) in his manager's car, and then run the last part of the race.

CHAPTER 16

STATISTICS
ANALYTICS AND THE A'S

Billy Beane, general
manager of the
Oakland Athletics

A measly $40 million. In the world of major league baseball, that's way too little to build a winning team. And yet, in 2002, that's exactly what the owner of the Oakland Athletics is expecting his general manager, Billy Beane, to do. How is he supposed to compete against Boston and the Yankees when they're spending three times as much? And how is he supposed to make up for the fact that, with all those bucks, those teams have just lured away his three best players?

But Beane has some new ideas. He uses them to find a bunch of new players—guys he thinks will be solid, despite the fact that other managers haven't noticed them—and he signs them up for peanuts. (Baseball players come a lot cheaper when teams aren't fighting over them!) And Beane is right about how good the players are. In September, the A's set an American League record by winning 20 games in a row, and they make the playoffs when they win the American League West. What's more, they do it all without blowing the budget.

MAJOR LEAGUE BASEBALL – 2002 PAYROLL BUDGETS

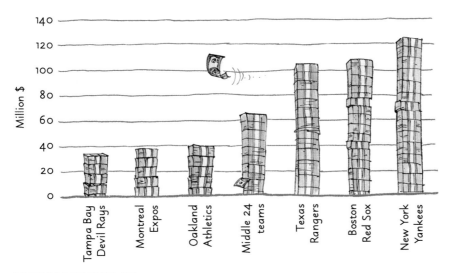

Only two teams had less to work with than Billy Beane's Oakland Athletics.

HOW HE DID IT

How did Beane beat the odds? He did two things differently from other major league managers. He didn't take his scouts' advice, and he relied heavily on statistics to find players.

All major league teams employ baseball scouts. They travel around, watching a few games at high schools, colleges, and minor league ballparks, checking out star players. They use stopwatches and radar guns to test running and pitching speeds. Then they tell the managers which players to sign. Most managers listen.

Not Billy Beane. Beane didn't believe that the scouts were as smart as they thought they were. He didn't believe scouts could know who would be successful just by watching a couple of games, and he thought they paid too much attention to how a player looked.

Scouts never recommended players who were overweight, or too skinny. And they didn't have much time for short players, either.

Beane thought statistics were a much better way to evaluate a player's potential. Stats had always been a big part of baseball, so relying on them was nothing new. But Beane used *different* stats from the rest of the league. He was sure that by looking at the right statistics over the whole season, he could predict a player's performance on the field better than a scout watching a few games. So instead of relying on his scouts, Beane relied on a statistician with a laptop computer. He used analytics—the systematic computing and analyzing of data—to find good, cheap players. In the process, he changed a lot about how baseball managers do their job.

WHY OBP BEATS BA

Time for some heavy-duty baseball talk! To understand how Beane did what he did, we need to look more closely at how a few statistics work. Let's start with what may be the most common baseball statistic of all—the batting average, or BA. At the time of Beane's big shift toward analytics, most teams used batting average to find good batters. Beane, though, preferred to look at on-base percentage, or OBP. He felt it was a much better measure of a player's potential. He went looking for players with good OBPs but poor BAs (because other teams wouldn't want them).

Why does it work? Look at the stats for two players in the same game:

Player 1	Player 2
5 plate appearances 2 singles 0 walks 3 strikeouts Total at bats: 5	5 plate appearances 1 single 2 walks 2 strikeouts Total at bats: 3*

* In the world of baseball stats, a walk counts as a plate appearance but not as an official at bat.

Now, let's do the math. **Batting average** is calculated by dividing the number of hits by the number of at bats: $H \div AB = BA$. So, how do our two players compare?

BA Player 1	BA Player 2
$2 \div 5 = .400$	$1 \div 3 = .333$

It's clear that Player 1 has a better average. But Beane believed that something about that statistic didn't make sense. Look again at the summary of what each player accomplished during the game. Player 1 reached base twice, while Player 2 reached three times. In Beane's mind, Player 2 helped his team more: getting on base three times is better than getting on base twice. And that's not all. Beane believed that a walk was extra-valuable to the team; if you don't swing at balls outside the strike zone, you force the opposing pitcher to throw more—raising his pitch count and tiring him out sooner.

All of this explains why Beane preferred **on-base percentage**, which takes those valuable walks into account. OBP is calculated by adding walks and hits and dividing that total by at bats plus walks (the short form for walks is BB, for base on balls): (H + BB) ÷ (AB + BB) = OBP. How do our two players compare this time?

OBP Player 1	OBP Player 2
2 hits + 0 walks = 2	1 hit + 2 walks = 3
÷	÷
5 at bats + 0 walks = 5	3 at bats + 2 walks = 5
=	=
.400	.600

Now who's looking like the more valuable player?

WHAT'S UP WITH THE WALKS?

In the 1840s, a group of people got together to define the first baseball statistics. One of them was British-born journalist Henry Chadwick. Chadwick grew up playing cricket and didn't really understand baseball. In cricket, there's no downside to swinging at and missing a ball that's not on target, so Chadwick didn't realize how much skill and discipline a baseball batter needs in order not to swing at a ball outside the strike zone. He thought that a walk on four balls was simply a pitching error. When he specified how to calculate batting average, he just removed walks. It's a mystery why people followed Chadwick's definitions for so long. For 150 years, very few people noticed that batting average isn't the best way to measure batters.

Information about walks is useful for more than just *finding* good batters. All season long, Beane monitored the number of walks that his batters were getting. If they weren't racking up enough, Beane would be all over them, yelling at them for swinging too often at balls outside the strike zone.

Baseball fan Bill James in the Kansas City stadium

A DEBT TO BILL JAMES

The type of analysis that Billy Beane relied on when rebuilding his Oakland Athletics is called sabermetrics (from SABR—the Society for American Baseball Research). Beane didn't invent sabermetrics. The guy who gets credit for that is Bill James. James wasn't a professional statistician or a baseball pro. He was just smart. After completing a college degree in economics and literature, James worked as a night watchman in a pork and beans factory. In 1977, he started

BOSTON RED SOX WORLD SERIES WINS

1903 1912 1915 1916 1918

←— 85 Years! —→

HIRE BILL JAMES

2003 2004 2007 2013

publishing an annual collection of his essays on baseball statistics. He had only a handful of readers at first, but in the 1980s, it became a bestseller.

Baseball fans loved James's ideas, but very few in professional baseball paid any attention. Billy Beane was different. He read every word that James wrote. After Beane's success with Oakland in 2002, the Boston Red Sox tried to hire him for a huge salary. He turned them down, so the Red Sox hired Bill James instead. Looking at their record of World Series wins, that was a smart move.

In many ways, that 2002 season changed baseball. When a book called *Moneyball* told the story of Beane and the Oakland A's, it got a lot of publicity (and was later turned into a movie). Other major league teams started paying more attention to the same statistics that Beane was using. These days, pretty much every team has its own statistician—and, as a result, it's become harder to find good players who are undervalued. Even so, Billy Beane has found new ways to do just that, and his Oakland A's have consistently continued to beat teams who have much bigger budgets.

STATS OVER SCOUTS: A PERSONAL CHOICE

Billy Beane was a brilliant high-school athlete. He was big, strong, and fast. As a 15-year-old sophomore (second year), he was the football quarterback, the top-scoring basketball player, and a baseball star—as both a pitcher and a batter. Baseball scouts fell over each other to get their teams to hire him; he was drafted by the New York Mets.

For 10 years, he played mostly in the minor leagues, and also for the Mets, the Minnesota Twins, the Detroit Tigers, and, finally, the Oakland A's. He had all the physical talent in the world, and everyone kept expecting him to shine. But Beane just didn't have the right mental attitude. He threw temper tantrums when he made mistakes, and then he was awful for the rest of the game. He lost confidence in his own ability and started hitting too cautiously. At batting practice, when it didn't matter, he was a star. But on the field, it never happened.

Years later, when he became a general manager, he remembered how wrong the scouts had been about him and decided that sabermetrics was a better way to evaluate players.

Billy Beane didn't believe that the scouts were as smart as they thought they were.

OTHER SILLY STATS

Baseball is a game full of statistics—some more useful than others. Here are a few examples of stats that can leave the scorekeepers, and the fans, scratching their heads.

ERRORS:

It's pretty hard to measure fielder performance. The most common measure is errors—noted with a capital *E* on the score sheet. The fewer errors, the better the fielder is supposed to be. When one of those *E*s shows up, it means that the official scorer has decided that a fielder misplayed the ball and has either allowed a runner to advance or a batter to reach base safely when they should have been out. The problem with this is it's all just an opinion. In baseball terms, an error usually means dropping or fumbling the ball. But you have to get to the ball in the first place to do that. Usually, *that* means the fielder has done something right—he's made it a close play. So, a good fielder might get charged with an error on a play where a weaker fielder wouldn't even have gotten there!

EARNED RUN AVERAGE (ERA):

The ERA—a measure of how many runs a pitcher allows per nine-inning game—is the most common pitching stat. The lower the ERA, the better the pitcher is supposed to be. What's up with the "earned" part? The idea is to measure only the pitcher's performance, so runs that score because of a fielding error don't count. But there are a couple of problems with ERAs. We just saw that a capital-*E* error isn't necessarily a real error. Also, singles, doubles, and triples are all influenced by fielders (even if no errors are assigned). Batters will get fewer runs against really good fielders than against weak fielders. That doesn't mean the pitcher is better, but it does mean he'll have a lower ERA.

Voros McCracken, a baseball fan who worked in a law office, came up with a better measure. It was called defense-independent ERA (dERA). It measures only strikeouts, walks, and home runs. Fielders have nothing to do with these.

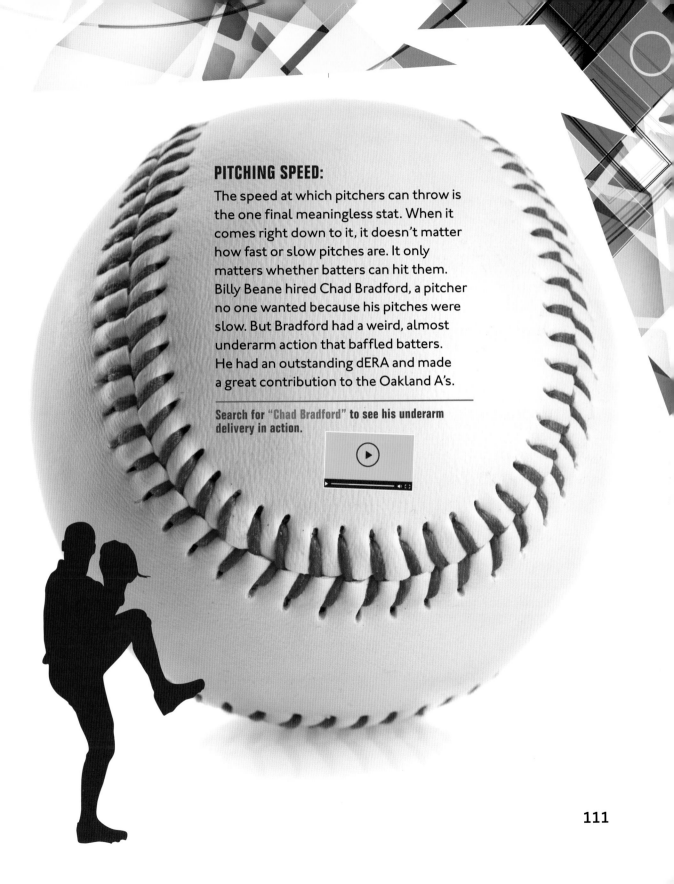

PITCHING SPEED:

The speed at which pitchers can throw is the one final meaningless stat. When it comes right down to it, it doesn't matter how fast or slow pitches are. It only matters whether batters can hit them. Billy Beane hired Chad Bradford, a pitcher no one wanted because his pitches were slow. But Bradford had a weird, almost underarm action that baffled batters. He had an outstanding dERA and made a great contribution to the Oakland A's.

Search for "Chad Bradford" to see his underarm delivery in action.

CHAPTER 17

BASKETBALL MICHAEL JORDAN'S HANG TIME

Occasionally, an athlete comes along who is so extraordinary that people are convinced he or she is doing something new and different. But as an old song says, "It ain't necessarily so." Michael Jordan was that kind of athlete. Millions of basketball fans around the world watched him in awe, certain that he'd invented a whole new way to play the game. In fact, he was playing the game the same old way as his teammates and competitors; he was just playing it better.

THE GREATEST OF THE GREAT

When you're a 6-foot-6 amateur basketball player, it's pretty easy to sink a shot. You just jump up, get your hands above the rim, and dunk the ball into the net. If you're a professional, though, that same move isn't quite so easy. The problem? You're likely to have someone who's more than 7 feet trying to block that shot.

Being able to work around those defenders is what separates the average players from the greats—players like Magic Johnson, Shaquille O'Neal, Larry Bird, and Kobe Bryant. But when it comes to the greatest of the great, one name is mentioned above all others: Michael Jordan.

Jordan played professional basketball from 1984 to 2003 (with a brief retirement between 1998 and 2001). For most of that time, he was a star shooting guard for the mighty Chicago Bulls. The team did well during Jordan's playing career, and Jordan himself collected numerous awards and honors. Fans went out of their way to watch this guy on the court.

What made Jordan so special? To start, he seemed to have a good strategy for making his shots. He would jump up into the air and let the defenders do the same. But then he would just stay up there, apparently waiting for his opponents to fall back down. Once that happened, he would dunk the ball before coming back to earth. As one professional player described it, "He goes up, stops for a cup of coffee, looks over the scenery, and then follows through with a tomahawk jam [a two-handed dunk]."

No wonder he's sometimes called "His Airness!"

Search for "NBA Michael Jordan 1988 Slam Dunk Contest." You'll find a video showing amazing slam dunks by Jordan, including one where he jumps from the free-throw line—22 feet from the basket—and still dunks the ball!

HOW HE DID IT

For years, Jordan made his trademark move look innovative and easy—so much so that people often wondered just what he did that was different. One of his coaches thought he had an explanation: "Simple," he said. "Michael Jordan is from another planet." It's a nice theory, but the truth is that Jordan didn't actually hover in the air. He just made it look that way.

Like everything else in the universe, Michael Jordan's body obeyed Sir Isaac Newton's law of gravity and laws of motion. Those laws tell us that gravity—which pulls you down to Earth—will slow you down if you're traveling upward and speed you up if you're traveling downward. Makes sense, right? But Newton's laws also let us in on another neat bit of information: the change of speed is constant. It doesn't matter if you're heavy or light, or what speed or direction you're traveling. Your speed will change by 32 feet per second with each passing second. If you take off upward at a speed of 32 feet per second, you will have slowed to 0 feet per second after one second has gone by. And after one more second,

you'll land back on the ground, traveling at—you guessed it—32 feet per second.

Back to basketball. Michael Jordan was able to jump upward at a speed of about 16 feet per second—half of the 32 feet per second that Sir Isaac's laws of motion identified. What this means is that after half a second, Jordan's upward speed was 0. After another half a second, he landed back on the ground. Newton's laws can also be used to calculate the height of his jump, which maxed out at 4 feet. That means that Jordan's face, which started at 6½ feet, maxed out at 10½ feet—above the 10-foot-high net! Holding his hands above his head put them way higher than the rim.

What do Newton's laws have to say about a jump that's not straight up? What if Jordan jumps at a 45-degree angle, so that he starts moving upward at 16 feet per second and at the same time across the court at 16 feet per second? Turns out, he would keep moving horizontally at the same speed while he's in the air. Putting all of these numbers together, we can calculate a graph of his trajectory (how he moved in the air).

Of course, all of this is true of all jumpers. Why did Michael Jordan seem to hover? Because:

- ○ **He could jump higher than almost all other players. That kept him in the air a little longer.**

- ● **He lifted his feet while in the air, which made it seem like he was higher than he actually was.**

- ● **He waited to dunk the ball until he was on the way down, as opposed to sinking the ball when he was at the peak of his jump. (Raising the ball as he was falling made it look as though he was hovering.)**

So, is Jordan's amazing hang time an innovation? Not really. But he sure made it look like one—and it was a whole lot of fun to watch!

HEIGHT AND DISTANCE

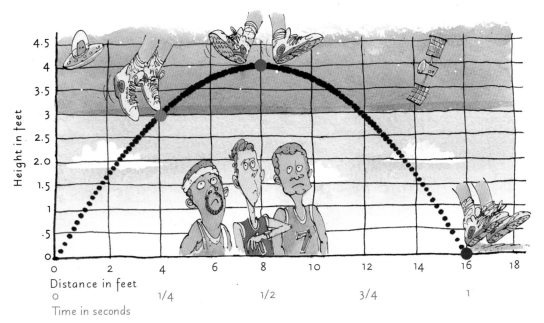

After a quarter of a second, Jordan's shoes are already 3 feet off the ground and he has moved 4 feet horizontally. His upward speed has slowed from 16 feet per second to 8 feet per second. His speed horizontally hasn't changed. It's still 16 feet per second.

Another quarter second takes him to his maximum height of 4 feet. By now, he's traveled 8 feet horizontally and is still traveling at 16 feet per second in that direction. His upward speed has slowed to 0.

After a full second, Jordan is back on the ground, 16 feet away from where he started.

If you look at the graph again, you'll notice that more time is spent in the higher part of the jump. For half of the air time (from the quarter-second mark to three-quarters of a second), Jordan is above 3 feet. This adds to the illusion of hovering in the air.

115

A SHOO-IN FOR ENDORSEMENTS

Many of the best athletes in the world are paid millions of dollars to play. Some are paid much more for endorsing (advertising) products like sports equipment and clothing. None of them has earned as much as Michael Jordan. The sportswear company Nike paid to use his name on their Air Jordan shoes and their Jordan brand clothing. More than a decade after he retired as a player, it's estimated that Jordan continues to earn close to $100 million a year from endorsements.

BASEBALL TOO?

Michael Jordan was such a talented athlete that he could have been a professional baseball player as well. Wait! He *was* a professional baseball player as well. After 10 years with the Chicago Bulls, Jordan retired from basketball. For two years, he played (mostly minor league) professional baseball. Then he went back to the Bulls for another three years.

April 1994: Michael Jordan batting for the Chicago White Sox in one of his few major league games.

MAIN SOURCES

Creighton, Joyce. *Boomerangs, Blades and Basketballs*. Austin, Texas: Steck-Vaughn, 2000.

Davis, Susan, and Stephens, Sally. *The Sporting Life*. New York: Henry Holt and Company, 1997.

Denny, Mark. *Gliding for Gold*. Baltimore, Maryland: The Johns Hopkins University Press, 2011.

Fosty, George and Darril. *Black Ice*. New York: Stryker-Indigo Publishing, 2004.

Friedman, Steve. *The Agony of Victory*. New York: Arcade Publishing, 2007.

Haché, Alain. *The Physics of Hockey*. Baltimore, Maryland: The Johns Hopkins University Press, 2002.

Hackett, A. J. *Jump Start*. Auckland, New Zealand: Random House New Zealand, 2006.

Lewis, Michael. *Moneyball*. New York: W. W. Norton & Company, 2004.

Moore, Richard. *The Dirtiest Race in History*. London: Bloomsbury Publishing, 2012.

Obree, Graham. *Flying Scotsman*. Boulder, Colorado: VeloPress, 2005.

St. John, Allen, and Ramirez, Ainissa. *Newton's Football*. New York: Penguin Random House, 2013.

ACKNOWLEDGEMENTS

Thanks are due to many people. To Rick Wilks and his team at Annick Press for giving me the opportunity to do this and for lots of help and encouragement along the way. To my amazing editor Linda Pruessen, who made the book come alive, who asked lots of hard questions that improved the book, and who was a delight to work with. To Sheryl Shapiro, who helped me every step of the way and whose graphic design magic made it look so good. (What a bonus to be married to your book designer!) To Ron Jenks, who gave me the full story behind fiberglass vaulting poles and who generously shared original documents. To AJ Hackett Bungy New Zealand for immediate, friendly responses and willing help. To many friends and family for assistance and encouragement—especially Rick Robbins, who also suggested the Ted Williams topic, Naomi Fromm, and Diane Lavi. To Jonah Wineberg and Benjamin Low for being intrepid age-appropriate testers of early versions. Thank you, all.